# T R U E

# UFO

# STORIES

# TRUE UFO STORIES

Terry Deary

*Illustrated by*

David Wyatt

Hippo

This book is dedicated to Brian Barrass,
who knows there is something out there.

Scholastic Children's Books,
Commonwealth House, 1–19 New Oxford Street
London WC1A 1NU, UK

A division of Scholastic Ltd
London ~ New York ~ Toronto ~ Sydney ~ Auckland

Published in the UK by Scholastic Ltd, 1997

ISBN 0 590 13448 5

Typeset by Rapid Reprographics Ltd
Printed by Cox & Wyman Ltd, Reading, Berks

10 9 8 7 6 5 4 3 2 1

# CONTENTS

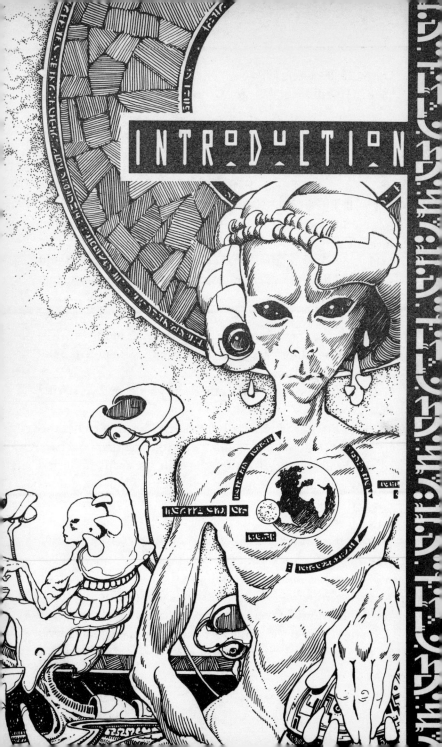

# INTRODUCTION

## Date: 15 January 1996
## Place: Burnhope Village, County Durham, England

On this winter morning I see my first UFO. The sun has not quite risen but it is just below the ridge a mile away, and it lights the sky a bright blue, like stone-washed denim, while the ground is still shaded a dark winter green.

I walk this stretch of road most days at this time. The dog trots along on its lead, exploring the scents of the quiet roadside verge while I look up at the sky. This morning I look over the valley to the distant woods, black-shadowed and sleeping. I look at the clear, glowing sky and wait for the first flash of the sun bursting above it.

But, this morning, I see something I've never seen before. Just above the trees there is a shape, hovering in the sky. It is the shape of a short, fat cigar. I guess it's less than five miles away and pretty large.

It doesn't move. It hangs there like a sleepy eye staring down at me.

I run. I'm not afraid, but I know that I need to record this sight. The confused dog thinks it's a game and drags me back to the house where I clatter through the front door and burrow into the cupboard under the stairs. I pull out a dust-covered camera case that hasn't seen daylight for a year, but I know it still has half a roll of film left in it. I rip at the zip and pull out the camera and lenses, hurry through the kitchen and throw open the back door.

The back of the house overlooks the woods that climb up to the distant ridge. The black cigar is still there staring, unwinking down at me. I raise the camera and find the shutter is jammed from neglect. I desperately tug at the winding lever to free it. Then I try to set the exposure correctly so the camera will be adjusted for the right light level. But the battery is flat and the exposure meter dead.

I guess at the setting, point the camera in the direction of the hovering object and fire off a shot. Got it! Now I have time to think a little more about the settings. I try again. Unidentified object in the centre of the viewfinder, press the button gently and ... *click*!

Now I reach into my pocket and pull out a telephoto lens. It's a little like fitting a telescope on the front of the camera. I screw the long lens on carefully. It makes the camera heavy and unsteady to hold. I rest it against the cold, winter-damp paintwork of the door frame and look through the viewfinder.

Now I can see the unidentified object as if it is just a few hundred metres away ... and I see it for what it is. It's a small gas-filled airship with a control cabin slung below it. I snap it anyway.

Nothing unidentified about it now ... nothing mysterious and nothing alien. Like most unidentified flying objects – UFOs – this sighting can be explained. It is explained as a mistake on the part of the witness.

Most sightings are like that.

Most . . .

But once in a while – probably about once in every *fifty* sightings – there is something that *cannot* be explained so easily. It is these one-in-fifty sightings and reports that make many people believe there is something more than harmless balloons up in our skies looking down. Unidentified flying objects that can't be explained as human or natural.

And, if they are not human or natural then they must be from beyond the world we know. They must be alien.

Do such things exist? It's important for our future that we know if there are strangers out there and find out what they want. Here are some of the thousands of accounts that have been reported over the years – they have been retold as stories for your entertainment, but the "facts" are as someone told them. They are placed alongside a summary of facts from similar cases.

It's up to you to decide if they are true from the facts you are given. Unless, of course, you have seen a UFO yourself and have already made up your mind . . . there is something out there watching us, and it isn't human!

*Many people think that alien visitors in their high-tech space craft began arriving fifty years ago. It's true that the term "flying saucer" was first used in 1947 to describe their mystic machines. But alien visitors go back a lot longer than that. This story is from 1926 . . .*

I know it happened eighty years ago when I were a lad of seven, but I remember it clear as yesterday. I've always had what they call a photographic memory. I close my eyes and I can see it.

It was November and the streets were cool and misty. The gas-lamps had haloes round them just like the pictures of saints in the old school books. The lads started to gather on the street corner after we'd had our teas, same as always. Just the lads – playing with lasses was soft in the north of England in those days. Lasses stayed indoors and helped their mams or played with dolls. But lads played out on the streets.

Albert Coleman was only nine years old but he was a big lad and we all took a lead off him. "What's it to be tonight, Albert?" I asked. "Cricket in the back lane?"

He planted his hands on the hips of his short grey trousers and scowled at me. "Cricket? In November? You haven't got the sense you was born with, Henry Towler."

I was glad the mist was bringing the dark on early because the shadows hid my blushing face. "Football in the front street?" Richard Brown suggested.

"No!" Albert said sharply. "Police have put a stop to that since a window got broken in Mrs Ramsbottom's chip shop."

"That weren't us!" Little Eddie Reid sniffed – always had a sniff and a drip on the end of his nose even on a warm day. That night it was running like a tap.

"What I'm saying," Albert sighed, "is the police are checking up. Give it a couple of weeks and they'll have forgot about it. Then we can start again."

"So what can we play, Albert?" I asked.

"Hide and seek."

"Yeah!" an excited breath went round the group. "This lamppost here's the block," Albert explained. He pointed to four of the lads. "Us five'll go off and hide first. You five . . ." he said, pointing at the rest of us. "You count to fifty, then come looking."

"Ten – twenty – thirty – forty – fifty! Block!" Richard Brown cried.

Albert gave him a hard look. "Don't be stupid, Richard."

"Sorry, Albert."

"And no cheating and looking where we go, either. Eyes shut till you get to fifty," he ordered.

"And no cheating from you," Eddie Reid chirped. "No hiding in people's back yards 'cos we get wrong for going in there ... and no hiding in the graveyard neither!"

"Scared?" Albert sneered.

"Yeah!" I said and everybody laughed. In those days the churchyard was the only thing we were scared of. Nowadays the streets themselves are dangerous. Times change.

That was one of the best games we ever had, that night. Creeping up to a corner and peering round, looking for the ones that were hiding. Trying to spot them before they spotted you. The way your hair stood on end when you saw a shadow move and you knew you'd found one. Then the mad race back to the lamppost, screaming, "Block!" and laughing.

But it seemed no time at all before I heard the dreaded voice. "Hen-reeee!"

"Aw, no!" I moaned. "It's me mam!"

"Pretend you never heard," Eddie advised.

"I'll get a belt round the lug," I sighed. "She'll not let us come out tomorrow night neither."

I picked up my jacket that lay in the gutter and dragged it all the way down the gleaming cobbles to our front door. "Up the wooden hill to Bedfordshire," Mam snapped. I opened my mouth to argue but changed my mind and trailed up the stairs.

The room was cold and I didn't fancy putting those freezing pyjamas on so I just slipped my black boots off and climbed under the sheets. I'd forgotten to draw the curtains so the street lamp cast its flickering blue-white shapes across my pillow. Then there was the sound of the lads out playing. The clatter of the boots and clogs on the cobbles and the cries of "All in, all out!"

I couldn't get to sleep. I couldn't. I just had to get out there and finish the game. I still had my clothes on. I put my feet on the floor and picked up my boots. I tiptoed down the stairs and out of the door while my mam was gossiping to the woman from number 8. I put my boots back on and ran down the street. I knew I had at least a couple of hours before my dad got back from the pub and locked the door.

"Thought you'd gone home," Albert said, like some stern school teacher.

"Just for a plate of dripping and bread," I said and I joined in the game again. It seemed that all the usual hiding places had been found and the lads were going further away. Way past the church. Way past the graveyard where the trees collected the water and dripped it on to the gravestones like wet footsteps limping through the gloom.

I shivered and hurried on past our rows of streets and came to one that was well off any road I usually took. Corporation Row was the name.

The back lane was dark except for a splash of yellow light that spilled over the narrow alley. And, in that light spill, I saw a shadow move and heard a faint noise. In this round everyone was back except Albert. If I could spy him – cheating and hiding in a back yard – I could cry "I see yer!" and have a good start in the race back to the lamppost.

I tiptoed down the lane, keeping close to the rough, black, brick walls and wished my dad didn't put so many hobnails in the soles of my boots. At last I reached the back gate where the amber light flowed out. There was a curious humming sound coming from the yard. For the first time it came to me that it might *not* be Albert hiding there!

I peered round the gatepost and I *knew* it wasn't Albert. In fact I didn't know what it was that I was looking at. Something told me it wasn't human!

The curtains of the back kitchen were open – that's where the light was coming from – and three figures were peering in. They were all about as tall as my dad; I remember he said he was five foot eight inches, so that'll give you some idea. They were wearing metal helmets on top of their silver suits. Their boots were black and so were the packs they carried on their backs. The packs looked like Flash Gordon's rocket suits and tubes went from them to the helmets.

I think I was so surprised that I said a swear word ... if my mam had been listening she'd have belted my ear. But it made the three figures turn round and I was in for an even bigger shock. Their faces stared at me from behind the glass fronts to the helmets and they were nothing like I've ever seen before or since. They had black, slit eyes and a thin slit where the nose should be, but no mouths.

"Albert *warned* me not to go in back yards," I groaned to myself.

The middle one of the three looked a little taller than the others. It took a step forward and made some funny gurgling sound like dirty water going down a drain. I didn't stop to say, "Would you mind repeating that, I didn't quite catch what you said!"

I ran. Albert was running back to the lamppost . . . and Albert was the fastest runner in our street . . . but I sped past him. My boots were striking sparks off the cobbles as I skidded round the corner into our street. "Come on, Henry! You're beating him!" the lads cheered.

"Where's he off to?" little Eddie said as I clattered past him, ignored the lamppost and screeched over the cobbles to our front door. I tore my boots off, opened the door and scampered up the stairs like a rat with its tail on fire. I didn't bother with the pyjamas. I just threw myself into the bed and lay there quivering.

Some time later that night my dad stuck his head round the door. "Night, night! Sleep tight! Mind the fleas don't bite!" he called as he always did.

My jaw was locked too tight to reply. "Asleep," he hissed at my mam as they made their way to bed. Asleep? I thought I'd never sleep again.

Now it would have all been forgotten, and I'd have thought

I *dreamed* it but, next day in school, the master was talking about Christmas – just five weeks away. "And the Three Wise Men visited Jesus in the stable ..." he said.

And I said, "I've seen them!"

I don't know what made me say it. It just came out. "I saw the Three Wise Men in a back yard at Corporation Row."

At first the master threatened to belt me for taking the Holy Book in vain. But I started to tell him the story and it all poured out of me. I must have made it sound good because the whole class went quiet, listening to me.

Somehow word got out to the newspapers and the next night, while I was sitting down to some bread and jam and a mug of tea, a newspaper man came and interviewed me. I had my picture in the paper. People wrote in and said they'd seen strange lights in the sky that same night. My class talked about nothing else for days.

But it was what you call a seven day wonder. It was in the papers just before Christmas then all forgotten a few days later. Except there was something so funny happened that I believe to this day there was more to it than some childish fantasy.

Because, two days after Christmas there was a knock at the door. My dad was still on his Christmas holiday and he was sitting with his feet in the fireplace, smoking a pipe while my mam was knitting him a new pair of socks. The way he stuck his feet in the fireplace he got through a lot of socks did my dad.

"I wonder who that is?" my mam said.

"Only one way to find out," my dad said ... but he didn't move.

Mam put her knitting down, glared at dad and marched across to the door. I heard the voices in the passageway. "Mrs Towler?" a voice asked. A creaking, mechanical voice with a strange accent. "We are from the Ministry of War. I wonder if we could have a word with young Henry?"

"Why, come in, sir," I heard my mam say and she led the way into the living room. Two men in black suits followed her. Something about them made me shiver even though I was sitting on the rug in front of the fire. I was playing with my Christmas present – a wooden train set.

Mam pulled two chairs out from the dining table and the men sat on them. They were straight-backed as the chairs. Their faces were pale as the gas-light and their eyes colder than Christmas. One of the men put a black box on the table. The other did all the talking.

"Now, Henry," the man said. His lips hardly moved. Shiny, dark-red lips that hypnotized me. I couldn't take my eyes off them. "You've been telling stories to the newspapers, haven't you?"

"Yes, mister."

"But not *true* stories," the man went on and his mechanical voice was lower and somehow menacing. "You made them up."

"Now here! Our Henry's a wild lad, but he doesn't tell lies," my dad started to object but suddenly his jaw locked and he struggled to breathe. I noticed Mam was just as frozen with her knitting needles held in rigid hands.

"What happened, Henry," the man went on, "was that you fell asleep. You dreamed that you went out to play and you dreamed you met some strange men in silver suits."

"I didn't!" I objected.

"You did!" the man persisted. "You came up with the story because you knew you were in trouble for claiming to have seen the Three Wise Men. The teacher was angry. You made up the story."

"No! The lads all saw me. I went out again after ten minutes in bed."

"*So*! You disobeyed your parents! You made up this story so your parents would not punish you for slipping out of the house!" he said, louder now.

"I didn't!" I cried.

"You *did*! Have you any idea the panic you could cause by spreading silly rumours about invading aliens? Luckily no one will believe the word of a child," the man said and his voice dropped to a hiss. The red of his lips was beginning to smear like lipstick. His face was twisted and lopsided.

"It's the truth!" I wailed.

Suddenly he rose to his feet and said, "Let's go, number 376," and his partner with the black box rose to his feet and the two marched to the door and out of the house. The door slammed and they were gone.

Mam shook her head. "Well! I'll go to the foot of our stairs!" she exclaimed.

Dad looked at his lifeless pipe and blinked in a dazed sort of way. "You what?" he said.

Now as the years have gone by I may have doubted what I saw in Corporation Row that night. But the visit from those two men in black suits convinced me that I *did* see something. Something I shouldn't have seen.

Something that was from out of this world.

And if I live another seventy years I'll never forget the night I met the three wise aliens.

## Men in Black – FACT FILE

One feature of stories about aliens and UFOs is the addition of a tale about men in black suits appearing and questioning witnesses. They seem to be checking on just what happened.

Experienced UFO watchers are so familiar with these strange visitors they have a nickname for them. MIB ... Men In Black.

**1.** Occasionally there are three Men In Black who visit the witnesses of a UFO appearance. But in most cases there are just two men. Normally they can be identified by their black suits but occasionally an unexplained questioner has turned up in a military uniform. Witnesses seem more willing to talk when faced by someone they think is a senior military officer.

**2.** People who have been visited by MIB agree that their aim seems to be to get witnesses to agree to a simple explanation of the sighting. They suggest that the witness made a mistake or saw some familiar object from an unusual angle. If the witness argues then the MIB can become very agitated and angry. When they fail they may leave suddenly and walk away without another word.

**3.** In many MIB appearances the strangers are driving a luxurious car – a Cadillac in the USA or a Jaguar in the UK. They often carry identity cards to show that they are from the Ministry of Defence (in Britain) or US Intelligence services. Sometimes their message is quite simple; in Maine, USA in 1975 a Man In Black simply said, "Better keep your mouth shut if you know what's good for you."

**4.** MIB don't simply make threatening visits. In 1953 a UFO expert, Albert Bender, claimed he was kidnapped by MIB and taken to the Antarctic. There he was so afraid of being left to freeze he agreed to keep quiet about his UFO knowledge. He kept his promise until 1960 when, he says, the MIB left Earth for their home planet and he was free to talk. A British witness was simply taken to some marshes on

the Borders of Scotland ... but when he proved unhelpful the MIB left him there with a five-mile walk home. It could have been worse, he could have had to walk home from the Antarctic!

**5.** If the MIB left Earth in 1960 then they didn't stay away for long. There were many reports of MIB activity between 1965 and 1967 and they were still being spotted in the 1970s.

**6.** The MIB are not to be trusted according to Albert Bender. They told him that the US Government knew all about UFOs and would tell the public the truth within five years. The five years came and went and there was no government announcement. Either the MIB lied ... or the government did.

**7.** If a Man In Black calls a companion something then he calls him a number, rather than a name. Sometimes the one who does the talking calls himself "The Commander".

**8.** MIB seem to be interested in asking questions about peculiar details of UFO witnesses' stories. For example, they may not ask about when or where the incident happened but they will ask at great length about exactly how the door of the space craft opened. But sometimes they are threatening; a Man In Black visitor offered fisherman Carlo Rossi a cigarette that tasted "bad" when he reported seeing a UFO in Italy in 1952 – was it poisoned? Rossi survived the cigarette, but died when he was knocked from his bicycle by a hit and run driver.

**9.** Sometimes the MIB are WIB! Women In Black have been reported in the USA. In a 1976 case in Maine the MIB and WIB had to leave suddenly because the WIB announced that her power was running low.

**10.** There have been cases where the MIB has turned out to be a *fib* . . . or even an FIB – a Fake In Black! In 1982 a UFO group were warned to stop their activities (or else) by two MIB. The UFO group set a trap to catch the MIB on camera and they succeeded. The threatening man did not want to protect alien secrets – he wanted to steal them for his own people. He turned out to be a very human member of a rival UFO club!

**11.** By 1996 Men in Black were reported to be patrolling the skies in unmarked, black helicopters and have been seen all over the world. In the USA a teenager took close-up photographs of a UFO but the MIB helicopter swooped and the photographs were taken from him. And in the UK the MIB disintegrated a coin in the hand of a UFO witness; they warned her, "The same will happen to your heart if you talk!"

THE HILLS ARE ALIVE

*Every now and then a UFO report is received that is totally different from any other. Usually this is the start of a new series of reports from dozens of people. But the case of Betty and Barney Hill began a flood of claims that some believe could run into millions! The belief that you have been kidnapped by aliens …*

"There's someone out there. Watching you," the voice said.

The woman's hand trembled as she held the telephone. "Thank you," she whispered. "I knew I hadn't imagined it."

She replaced the telephone in its cradle and it rattled as she lowered it. The tall, brown-skinned man sat on the edge of the chair and looked at her with troubled eyes.

"Who?" he asked and his voice was hoarse.

The woman's face was pale and the jet hair framed it like a stiff curtain. "Probably humans," she murmured.

"So why don't they come to the house if they want to talk to us?"

As he said the words there was a sharp rap on the front door. The man and woman both jumped, stared at the door to the hall and froze. "You go, Barney," she said in a soft whine.

He rose from the chair with the stiffness of a machine and said, "I'll go, honey," as if he hadn't heard her.

He licked his lips as he carefully opened the door into the hallway and seemed to stand for an age with his hand on the catch of the front door. "Who's there?" he asked and his voice was a light croak from such a well-built man.

"Jess Winter, Mr Hill. You remember, I called on the phone and asked if it would be OK for me to call round tonight?"

"Who is it?" Betty Hill called from the living room.

"Mr Winter!" her husband called back. "From the UFO Society. Wanted to interview us. Remember?"

"I forgot," the woman said and gave a nervous laugh. "Let him in and I'll put the coffee on."

Barney Hill opened the door and let the young man in. He had a knapsack on his back and thrust out a small hand which Barney took into his bear-paw. "Pleased to meet you, Mr Hill. It's a privilege for me to be able to talk to you. You're probably the biggest names in ufology for twenty years!" he went on. He rubbed a hand nervously over his cropped hair and his pale eyes shone in the dim light of the hallway.

"Come in, Jess," Barney Hill said and led the way into the living room. A comfortable room, drab in colour but not poor.

Betty smiled from the kitchen. "Coffee's on. You just start asking your questions and I'll get on with it." She seemed happier moving around, rattling cups and fussing with the percolator.

Jess Winter cleared his throat. He was the most nervous of the three. "I don't want to twist your story by asking you questions. We find that asking questions gets the answers we're hoping for rather than the truth." Barney Hill nodded slowly. The young interviewer cleared his throat again and went on. "Maybe you could just tell your story from the start," he suggested as he scrabbled in his knapsack for a ballpoint pen and reporter's notebook.

Betty began and her voice was flat as she told a tale she had practically off by heart. "It was the night of 19 September 1961 and Barney and I were driving home from Montreal. We'd had a short holiday up at Niagara Falls and we were on our way home when it happened.

"We were driving home at night to save on another night's hotel bill. We stopped for a snack at around 10 p.m. in a place called Sherbrooke." Jess Winter rustled a map as he ran a finger down the road from Montreal. "Then we headed south down Highway US3. I guess we'd gone about thirty miles after that and hadn't seen another living soul – no cars, and any houses we passed were in darkness. That's when we saw a bright light in the sky."

"Who saw it first?" the interviewer asked.

Betty Hill came through from the kitchen with a tray and placed it on a low table in front of him. She shrugged. "It was so odd I guess we both saw it at the same time. A really bright light in the sky moving incredibly fast. Anyhow, we stopped and got out of the car with our binoculars."

"What did you see?" Jess Winter asked eagerly.

"I was coming to that," the woman sniffed. It was her story and she knew how to tell it. "It was flat like a pancake, I guess. It had lights along the front but not at the back, so as it spun round it appeared to be flashing. It also had a couple of fins at the edge that had red lights on them."

Barney Hill reached into his pocket and slid a piece of paper across the table a little shyly. "I did this sketch when you said you were coming."

"Thanks," the young man breathed. "This is wonderful, Mr Hill!"

Betty was impatient to get on with the story. "We stopped another twenty miles on and got out of the car again . . ."

"That would have taken you into the National Forest area," the ufologist interrupted, checking his map again.

"That's right. But now the pancake was hovering in front of us. Really close!"

"We weren't scared, were we honey?" Barney asked. "Even though we could see clear into those windows. I kept telling you, there had to be some explanation. I was staring at this UFO and telling you I do not believe in UFOs! But when they got close enough I could make out figures dressed in shiny black uniforms. I stared at one of them ... and realized that he was looking straight back at me. And *that's* when I got the weirdest feeling."

"Weird?"

"Scared. Like I wanted to run for my life." Barney trembled.

Betty gave a thin, tight-lipped smile. "He got back into the car crying, 'They want to capture us! They want to capture us!' He hit the floor with the pedal and we got the hell out of there," she said.

"That's when we heard the pinging sounds on the trunk of the car. Like they were firing at us. I guess I was more scared than I've ever been in my life."

Barney sipped his coffee while Betty simply clutched hers in both hands and stared at the floor. "We reported it to a UFO group about a week later," she said.

"And?" the young man urged. He knew this was just the start of the story.

"And . . . we repeated the story several times over the next couple of months. I was having dreams but I didn't think much about them at the time. Dreams about going inside of the space craft. But it wasn't till one of the UFO guys said, 'What took you so long to get home?' that it suddenly hit us. We'd *lost* at least two hours!

"That's when I started to take my dreams seriously. I realized that they could explain the missing two hours. We really *had* been inside the space craft."

Barney leaned forward. "I didn't remember it myself, but the UFO Society suggested I get myself hypnotized ... they reckoned it might unlock the memories in my mind."

Jess Winter nodded. "Tell me about the dreams," he said.

The woman's tired eyes became glazed as she stared at the young man's notebook. He wrote quickly as she spoke like a machine gun. "We get back in the car. We drive fast down the road. First we swing sharp left then sharp right. Then the headlights catch them. Eleven of them standing in the road. Shiny black uniforms. I want to hit them. Run them down. Break through their cordon. Escape. But suddenly the engine dies. The car stops itself. Barney turns the key but it's dead. We're trapped. Can't go backwards or forwards. They start to walk towards us! They're hideous. Two arms and two legs, but flat faces with two nostrils but no nose. Eyes like lizards'."

"They open the car doors," Barney said, picking up the story, "and they take us by the arm and lead us along a path through the woods."

"I'm speaking to you," Betty said. "You don't seem to hear me."

"I hear you," her husband replied and sweat began to trickle down his dark brow. "I just can't answer. Can't do anything but walk. They lead us to the space craft in a clearing."

"It's big. Big as this house," Betty continued. "We have to

climb a ramp to get inside. It's dark in there and I don't want to go in. I just don't seem in control."

"There's a corridor all the way round the outside of the craft," Barney explained. "Rooms lead off the corridor. They take Betty in the first room . . ."

"I want to know why Barney can't come inside with me," Betty cried, her face pale as the cream in the jug on the tray. "The leader tells me they only have one examination room. They'll take Barney next door and that will save time. Then he starts to ask me questions . . ."

"In English," Barney explained. "They spoke English."

"They ask me what I eat, how old I am and then they start to examine me. They take wax from my ears – clippings from my fingernails. They even scrape a patch off my skin." The woman rolled up her sleeve and showed a sore patch of dry skin on her forearm. "But it's worse when they push a huge needle into me. Say they want to examine me inside. I think I scream when I feel the needle ... then he waves a hand in front of my face and all the pain vanishes. I'm not even afraid any more."

"Don't forget, you ask him for proof, Betty," Barney said.

She nodded. "The leader shows me a map. Says it's a star map. Says it shows his home planet. I can still see that star pattern when I close my eyes. I sometimes look at the stars now and wonder where they are. Those strange creatures."

The couple fell silent. Finally Jess Winter said, "They took you back to the car."

Betty Hill looked at him strangely, like someone who's just woken in an unfamiliar room. "We ... we were back at the car, I remember. Then we looked towards the woods and we saw the pancake roll like a ball – it glowed and then vanished at an incredible speed."

"And then you drove home."

Betty took a deep breath. "I turned to Barney and said, 'Now do you believe in flying saucers?' Barney just said, 'Don't be ridiculous.' It seems like he forgot the whole thing as soon as he got back to the car. And I only remembered it ten days later when I started having the dreams. Except, of course, they turned out not to be dreams ... Barney saw the same things!"

"Did you tell Barney about the dreams?" the ufologist asked.

"Of course!" Betty exclaimed, surprised by the question. She placed three fingers on her lips. "You don't think he just listened to me talking about my dreams and started to believe them?"

"It's possible," Jess Winter said.

"But there are so many other weird things happening," she said quietly. She looked troubled. She spoke uncertainly. "There was a pile of leaves – dead leaves – on the kitchen table. I went to brush them off and saw something shining. Earrings – the earrings I was wearing on the night we were kidnapped."

"Anything else?"

"Silly things ..." Barney cut in. "But they never happened before. Lots of problems with electrical stuff. Toasters and refrigerators and radios and the television. The burglar alarm set itself off for no reason."

"No burglars?" the ufologist asked.

Betty looked at him and said, "Not the human kind. We've seen shapes moving in the shadows after dark. Just before you arrived my neighbour phoned to say she'd seen them too. Something prowling outside. They haven't finished with us yet, Mr Winter. They're still keeping an eye on us. There's someone out there now."

"Why, Mrs Hill?"

The woman moved to sit next to her husband. She gripped his hand till her knuckles were white. "Because they are coming back for us. Somewhere, some time, they are going to come back for us."

"And if they can't get you?"

"Then they'll take someone else. These creatures will be back. Believe me, Mr Winter. They'll be back. And the frightening thing is ... there's nothing we can do about it!"

### Alien Kidnapping – FACT FILE

The Hills' case was the first of many reports of aliens kidnapping humans, examining them then releasing them.

There is no real *evidence* that a human has ever been abducted by an alien but many people have sworn that it happened to them. It is hard to prove that you have been taken into a space craft: it is just as hard for someone to prove you are mistaken or lying. One person who looked closely at the story of Barney and Betty Hill said . . .

• They had seen the planet Jupiter, not a UFO.

• They changed the time of the sighting several times as they retold the story. It was "around 11 p.m.", it was "between midnight and 1 a.m." and it was "around 3 a.m."

• There was no "lost two hours". Barney had driven slowly and stopped several times and there was nothing odd about their time of arriving home.

• They said they walked a long way from the car to the UFO yet, after the examination, they walked a short way back to their car.

• Barney and Betty told different stories at different times. It was never clear if the aliens spoke English or if the Hills just "heard" the alien thoughts inside their heads.

Barney Hill died in 1969, five years after he

34

repeated his story to a hypnotist. Betty gave up work to become a full-time UFO expert. She told UFO watchers that she knew a place in New Hampshire where she would regularly see from 50 to 100 UFOs a night! Other investigators went with her and saw only aircraft landing lights or street lights in the distance. Common mistakes for someone setting out to look for UFOs.

The Hills may have started the rush of alien kidnap stories but they are not the most unusual.

**1.** Mrs Sandra Larson, her daughter and a friend were all taken aboard an alien craft and cut up like frogs in a biology lesson. The kindly aliens then put them back together again ... without leaving any scars!

**2.** In November 1979 two young Frenchmen reported that their friend had disappeared from their car when a glowing mist settled on it. The police searched for the friend but failed to find him so they arrested the two for his murder. Seven days later the missing friend appeared and said he'd just been asleep for half an hour. He had no idea where he'd spent the last week. When he was hypnotized he remembered meeting aliens who said they would be back on 15 August 1980. Hundreds waited for the aliens to reappear ... but they didn't turn up.

**3.** In December 1992 the Houston UFO Network (HUFON) planned to trap the alien

abductors. They hypnotized people who had been abducted before. The next time one was abducted she was able to say, "We know what you are doing! Let's talk about it." This really seemed to upset the aliens and caused them to abduct several more people in order to find out what was going on.

**4.** In 1956 a young American called Howard Menger met a group of space people. They let him listen to space music and sample a space potato. They told him that they came from the planet Venus. But the biggest surprise was when they told him he too came from Venus ... and so did his wife.

**5.** Hideichi Amano was driving up a mountain near Sayama City, Japan, in 1978 when he had a curious encounter. He was examined without even leaving his car. A round-faced alien stopped the car and it walked up to Amano with a tube in its mouth. The creature pressed the pipe against Amano's head and a babbling noise came from it. The man said he thought the alien was sucking the memories from his brain and the noise was like a tape recorder running at high speed.

**6.** Not all kidnappings are a success ... and not all use invisible rays to paralyse the humans. In 1954 near Caracas in Venezuela a gang of hairy aliens leapt from their hovering space craft and set

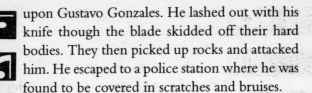

upon Gustavo Gonzales. He lashed out with his knife though the blade skidded off their hard bodies. They then picked up rocks and attacked him. He escaped to a police station where he was found to be covered in scratches and bruises.

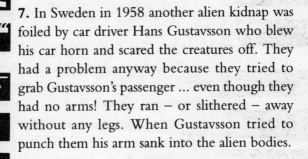

**7.** In Sweden in 1958 another alien kidnap was foiled by car driver Hans Gustavsson who blew his car horn and scared the creatures off. They had a problem anyway because they tried to grab Gustavsson's passenger ... even though they had no arms! They ran – or slithered – away without any legs. When Gustavsson tried to punch them his arm sank into the alien bodies.

**8.** Humans aren't the only Earth creatures in danger of alien abduction. In Wales in 1977 a herd of cattle kept disappearing when UFOs were sighted in the area. In Puerto Rico in 1980 some children watched a crew of aliens take a great interest in their flock of chickens in the farmyard!

**9.** Some people claim to have been abducted from their own beds – then returned safely without even knowing they've been and come back. They only remember when they are hypnotized. An American was paid $1 million for the story of his abduction in 1987. In 1993 he admitted he had made it all up. Still ufologists believe him; they also believe that the aliens have the power to transport human bodies through bedroom walls. But, if they are clever

enough to do that, why did they leave a door open when they left, as they did in Sheffield, England, in 1993?

**10.** A US hypnotist began putting his patients into a trance to see if they had been abducted then forgotten about it. Amazingly nearly everyone who visited him discovered they had been kidnapped in their sleep at some time. The hypnotist then announced that the number of Americans who had been abducted totalled an incredible 3.7 *million*! If that were true then hundreds of UFOs must be kidnapping hundreds of Americans every night! Where are all these aliens coming from? Why do they need so many victims? Surely they must know human beings inside out after 3.7 million tests? And why are they picking on Americans? If they are doing the same tests all over the world then there must be hundreds of thousands of UFOs whizzing around, kidnapping, testing and returning people to their beds. Amazing ... or ridiculous?

*Many people say, "If there are so many UFO sightings and alien landings, how come there is no evidence — no pieces of space craft, no alien bodies on Earth?" Ufologists argue there are remains of space craft that have crashed and aliens who have been killed in the crash. The trouble is that governments have kept it very quiet and hidden the truth from us. The most famous crash was in the USA, near a little place called Roswell ...*

A wind swept over the dry plains. It blew crows across the sky like black confetti and shook the stunted, leafless bushes. It looked like the loneliest place on Earth.

An old man appeared at the top of the ridge overlooking the rolling plain. He rested for a while on his stick and was joined a moment later by a boy.

The man's clothes were black as funeral ribbons and his face lined with grey furrows. Even his silver-topped walking cane was black. The boy stood a pace behind him. He raised his voice a little because the wind was sweeping his words away and because the old man was a little deaf. "Is this where it happened, Grandpa?"

The man's faded eyes watered as a small dust devil swirled by. There was a hollow in the earth where a bush had been torn from the dry land. He lowered himself into the shelter of the hollow and patted the ground, "Sit down, Joe."

The boy dropped to the ground and looked across the plain. The man raised his cane and pointed to a spot on the grey-green earth below. "It's overgrown now," he said. "But fifty years ago there was a deep scar like something had hit the ground at a terrific speed."

There was a shadow of a shadow on the earth. Joe thought he could make it out. "And that's where the flying saucer crashed?" he asked.

"Not exactly," the old man said. He spoke slowly and carefully. "Part of it crashed here – the main part of the cabin was found up north at Corona."

The boy shook his head. "I just can't understand it, Grandpa. These aliens travelled all the way across the universe to Earth so they must have been brilliant fliers."

"They must," the man agreed.

"So how come they manage to crash when they get here?" Joe asked. "They must have been pretty stupid or careless."

"Mmmm," his grandfather nodded. "As I remember there was a storm on 2 June that year ..."

"1947?"

"1947. The worst storm anyone can ever remember seeing. I certainly haven't seen a worse one since. Now the rancher that owned the land in 1947 was called Mac Brazel. He remembered seeing a great flash in the sky over this area. It was something red with a white tail but he guessed it was ball lightning or something. Then it was another four or five days before he rode out this way to check on his stock. And that's when he saw the groove in the ground and saw the wreckage."

"But not the dead bodies?"

"But not the dead bodies. He looked at the wreckage and found it looked like very thin metal. He could crumple it in his hand it was so thin and light. But when he opened his hand it sprang back to its original smooth shape, like magic."

"I don't believe in magic," Joe said. "And I don't believe in aliens."

His grandfather's face creased in a lopsided smile. "Neither did I! Oh, there'd been hundreds of UFO sightings that summer of '47. It was all over the newspapers. In fact there was even a reward offered for anyone finding proof of an alien landing. Three thousand dollars reward. Of course Mac Brazel thought he'd struck gold! He hauled away the biggest pieces of the wreckage and stored them in the barn next to his ranch house."

"I'll bet it's not there now," Joe sighed.

"No. Mac told the sheriff and he told the local radio station. But just before he went on air to announce that he'd found a flying saucer he lost his nerve. He said it was just bits of metal. Mac Brazel was scared by something . . . or somebody."

"Who, Grandpa? The aliens?"

"No ... most people reckon it was government secret agents that told him to keep quiet. We saw Mac around town in the next week but he always had people from the Roswell Air Base with him. It was like they were guarding him. The radio and newspapers were told to drop the story and they threw a guard around this whole site for miles. We couldn't get near."

"Did you try, Grandpa?"

"I tried, Joe. We folk in Roswell wanted to see the wreckage. But by the time the military let us in there wasn't a scrap left to be found. For the last fifty years people have searched here and still there's none of the magic metal to be found. The military must have searched every inch."

"But you saw the scar," Joe said.

"We saw the scar."

"How did they explain that?" Joe demanded.

"They said it was a weather balloon – they're made of a silvery foil stuff. They even had an airforce officer show reporters the wreckage they said they'd found. It was a weather balloon, of course, but they could easily have switched the real wreckage."

"So, there's no proof," Joe shrugged. "I told you there's no such things as flying saucers and aliens."

The old man rose stiffly and looked to the north. "You're forgetting, Joe. I may not have seen the flying saucer ... but I sure saw something that wasn't human."

Joe looked at him suspiciously. "You're kidding me?"

"No. I swear on the little bit of life I have left. I've seen an alien. Remember, it was the body of the space craft that crashed here. Over at Corona some archaeologists were out digging. While the military were guarding the wreckage here, the archaeologists came across the cabin of the space craft on a ridge over at Corona. Of course the military got to them in no time and shut them up the way they shut Mac Brazel up. And that's when they called me up."

Joe's grandfather began to walk slowly down the ridge towards the black car that was parked at the edge of the dirt road. The pale dust powdered the polished paintwork.

He opened the door and sat behind the wheel. Joe sat beside him quietly as he reversed the car, turned and drove steadily back down the dirt road. It took them twenty minutes to reach the nearest highway. "You can see why a crash in this area could stay undiscovered for four days or more," the old man said.

"Tell me about the aliens," Joe demanded.

"I got back to the chapel of rest around 4 p.m. and the phone was ringing. A man asked if I was Glen Dennis, the town undertaker, and I told him I was. Now he asked the strangest question. He asked me what was the smallest coffin we had in stock. I told him that four foot was the smallest. He asked me to keep some for him. Then he called me back another three or four times that afternoon. He wanted to know about preserving a body. What chemicals did I use and how could he move a body without damaging it? I told him I could tell better if I saw the bodies."

"And he let you?" Joe asked eagerly

His grandfather shook his head. "He refused. The only thing I could get from him was that the bodies had been exposed to the elements for a few days and were decomposing. Whenever I asked questions he refused to answer."

"So how did you get to see the aliens?" Joe persisted.

"Now you know what a hearse is, don't you Joe?"

"Yeah. It's the long car you use to carry bodies to funerals," the boy said.

"That's right. Now in 1947 there was a shortage of ambulances. The military often used to borrow my hearse to move hospital cases on stretchers."

"Creepy!" Joe shuddered.

The old man's stone-grey face creased. "Not really, Joe. The dead never hurt anyone." The boy thought about it and nodded. Glen Dennis went on, "Anyway the last call of the day was from the air base. They wanted a young airman collecting from the town hospital and taking back to the hospital on the air base. Their own ambulances were busy bringing something in from Corona."

"The aliens?"

"I guess so. They paid me well so I drove out, collected the guy and went to Roswell Air Base. There was a lot of activity there. Whole convoys of trucks bringing men back from the crash site we just saw. Huge staff cars with Generals so important they were weighed down with gold uniform braid and medals. I've never seen so many top people come to little Roswell."

The car cruised along the highway and the old man turned down a narrow road signposted "Corona". "I dropped the injured soldier at the hospital but I decided to go inside. There was a nurse in there I knew. I wanted to say hello while I was there ... maybe take her for a coffee."

His grandson grinned. "Did grandma know?"

"This was three years before I met your grandmother," Glen Dennis said sternly.

"That's OK. I won't tell her," Joe sniffed.

"As I was saying," the man went on. "I started to get out of the ambulance and go into the hospital. There were two military police at the door. I'd never seen guards on the hospital before but I didn't think too much of it at first. I wouldn't have gotten as far as I did if I hadn't parked in the emergency area. The doors were open to the military ambulances and that's where the wreckage was and there was a military policeman on each side. I saw all the wreckage. I don't know what it was but I knew there was something going on. There were a lot of very high-ranking officers there. They were really shook up. That's when I saw Selene ..."

"The nurse?"

"That's her. I expected her to give me a friendly 'Hello!' Instead she looked horrified. She said, 'How in the hell did you get in here? My God, you are going to get killed.' I was standing by the Coke machine to get us a Coke when this big red-headed colonel said, 'What's that son of a bitch doing here?' And he was looking at me! When I turned to look at him I saw he was standing at the door to an operating theatre. Everybody seemed to be standing round a body on an operating table. I just saw a glimpse of what was on the table .... and I've never seen anything like it."

"The alien?"

"I saw hundreds of bodies in my job as an undertaker ... but I've never seen anything like that. It was silvery grey, about your size but with spindly little legs and arms. But before I got a really good look these two military policemen grabbed me by the arms and carried me clear outside. I didn't walk, they carried me. And they told me to get my ass out of there. They even followed me back to the funeral parlour, called on me and told me, 'If you open your mouth you'll be put so far back in jail they'll have to feed you with beans through a bean shooter.'"

Joe gave a sharp laugh. His grandfather turned. "They meant it, Joe!"

"Were you scared?" the boy asked.

"Not so much scared as angry. I just laughed and said, 'Go to hell!' But later the sheriff called and told me they'd threatened him too. Said they would kill his whole family if he ever talked about what he saw."

"And what *did* he see?" Joe asked.

"He never did say," Glen Dennis shrugged. "But Selene did. I phoned her at the hospital and arranged to meet her at a coffee bar that night. She finished at 10p.m. and when I met her she was really nervous. She could hardly hold the coffee cup without spilling some."

"She'd seen them?"

"She said, 'There were three bodies. Two of them mangled beyond everything but there was one of them that was really in pretty good condition. Really what they looked like was ancient Chinese. They were frail and small and had no hair. Their noses didn't protrude and their eyes were pretty deep and their ears were just indentations. They didn't have thumbs . . . just four fingers like tentacles with suction caps on the end.' The nurse drew a picture of the creatures but burned it because she was scared of what they'd do to her if they found it."

"I thought there were four bodies," Joe frowned.

"Three dead and one alive," the old man said carefully. "At least that's one of the rumours that went around. The nurse just saw the dead ones they were examining. But someone noticed some movement when they unpacked the bodies. They put the living alien in a sort of intensive care unit. It died later."

The undertaker stopped the black car on a ridge. The rock was bare and polished by the wind and sand. "Fifty years ago, Joe, four aliens crashed here. At this very spot. I can't prove it – the government has always denied it. I've seen lots of deaths but none as sad as those. We could have talked to beings from the other side of the universe. Learned the secrets of space travel from them! Who knows where we could be today?"

"Yeah, that's sad," the boy agreed.

"No," the old man said and rested on his cane. "What I meant was I was sad for those aliens. It's always bad when someone dies away from home and their loved ones. But no one on Earth has ever died as far from home as those poor creatures."

The boy stood silent and looked across the plain.

"I promised to show you the sites," his grandfather said quietly.

Joe nodded. "Thanks, Grandpa ... but I want to go home now."

## Little Grey Men – FACT FILE

Ever since the first flying saucer excitement of 1947 there have been rumours that UFOs have crashed and that the US Government has stored the wreckage. Some ufologists even claim that the alien pilots are still alive.

Reports of crashed UFOs have since come from all over the world. One was said to have been spotted in Russia in 1988 – but it vanished before the aircrew who spotted it could land and collect it. Another crashed on Mount Chitpec in Mexico but was claimed by the local Chaulas Indian tribe, who took it away, claiming it was a gift from God! In Bolivia in 1978 a crashed UFO caused such a huge explosion that it was recorded as an earthquake – though no wreckage was found to prove the story.

Aliens have been reported arriving in all shapes and sizes. But many ufologists now think there are just a few types of alien and the most common type have been named the "Greys". It was four "Greys" that were supposed to have crashed at Corona near Roswell.

**1.** The Greys are the aliens that most commonly kidnap (or abduct) humans, take them aboard space craft and examine them. They seem very curious about the way the human body works.

**2.** Greys are said to have a skull larger than a human's but a spindly and short body. Some ufologists believe that they can "talk" to one another by reading thoughts. To transmit and receive thoughts (like a radio service) they need a bigger brain and hence a bigger head.

**3.** The shade of their skin varies in different reports. Some are light tan, some white and others are different shades of grey. Just like humans it may be possible for them to have different skin colours yet all be the same species. It's harder to explain why some have noses and others don't!

**4.** Greys have thin mouths because they do not eat and they do not talk – the mouth is just a breathing hole so it is small and has no lips.

**5.** Greys don't show much feeling so humans often describe them as "cruel". Some are even reported to have killed and eaten humans, but that is very rare.

**6.** The most unusual belief is that the Greys are just servants of a greater and more terrible race of aliens: Giant Lizards or *Reptoids*. The Greys are preparing the way for the Lizards who used to live here in the days of the dinosaurs and are

now about to return. The Reptoids come from the Draco constellation and are fond of human flesh. The good news is that there's no evidence for this strange belief and it is not worth worrying about dinosaurs under the bed!

**7.** In the Roswell story (above), undertaker Glen Dennis said he'd seen a Grey being cut up and examined by doctors. In 1995 a film of the cutting up appeared on television. The film-maker said it was genuine and made a lot of money from selling copies. Most sensible people know it is in fact a fake. There is no proof that Greys have ever crash-landed – just stories.

**8.** Some astronomers claim to know where the Greys come from. They come from a planet around the stars Zeta Reticuli. The Greys that kidnapped the Hills showed Betty a star map. She remembered it in her dreams and sketched it. Astronomer Marjorie Fish said that the map was a perfect match for the Zeta Reticuli star system. She did not explain why aliens needed "road maps" of the stars when no space-ship journey could ever be planned with them.

**9.** Many ufologists believe the Greys have made an evil deal with world governments. The Greys give the governments scientific secrets – the governments allow the Greys to go on kidnapping their humans.

**10.** Luckily there are a group of aliens known as the Blues who are much more friendly and peaceful. They are supposed to be talking to the US Government about a treaty – but the only people who have signed a peace treaty with the US Government seem to be the Hopi Indians.

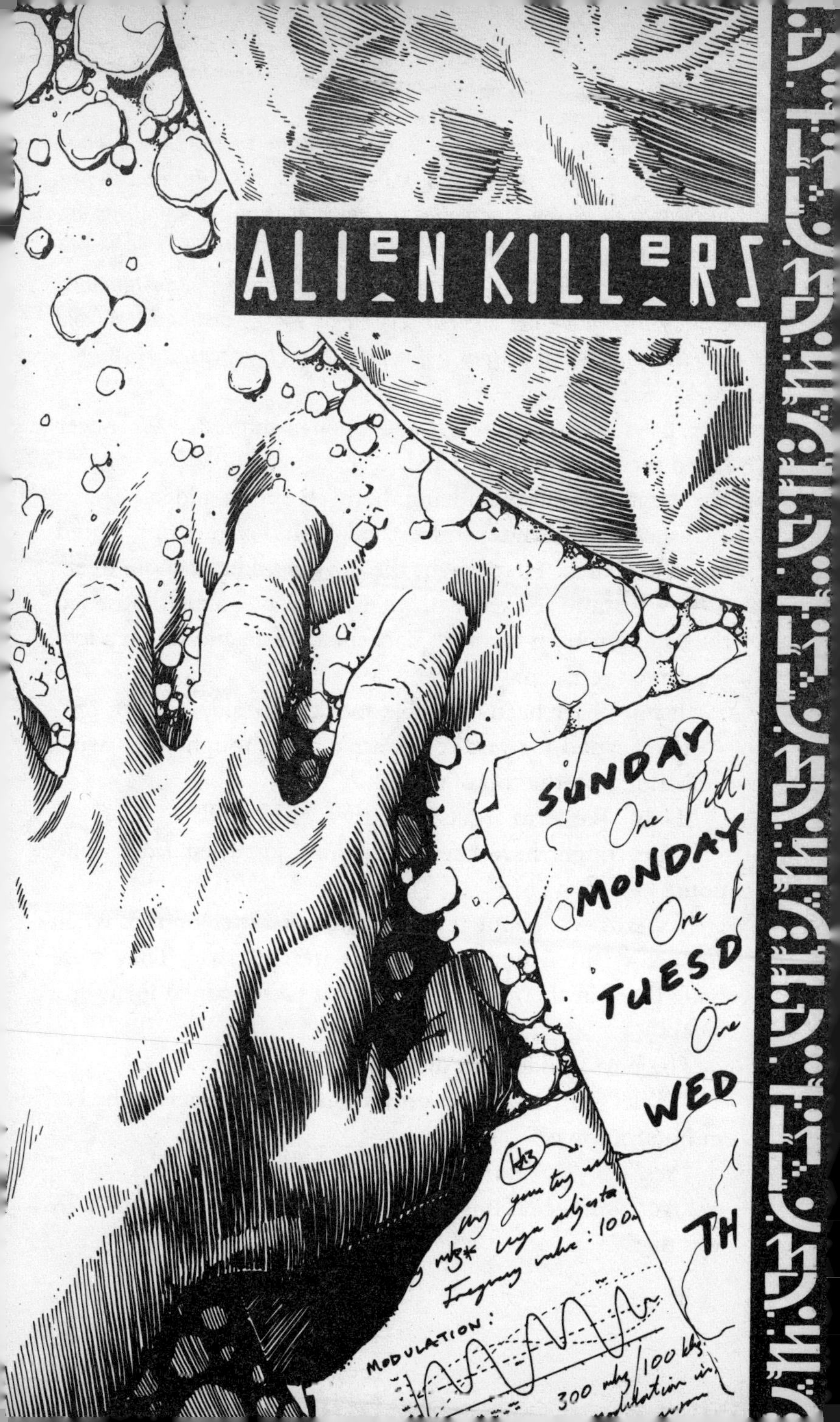
ALIEN KILLERS
SUNDAY
MONDAY
TUESD
WED
TH
MODULATION:

*A curious thing about UFOs is that they are so shy. Many have tremendous powers and can travel the universe yet they seem to run away as soon as someone points a camera at them. Some aliens are helpful and are thought to be "Angels" looking after suffering humans. But others are more devilish and actually harm humans. One of the most cruel cases, in Brazil in 1976, involved a double murder by person or persons unknown . . . or by aliens.*

The boys were wide-eyed and open-mouthed. "We never killed them!" Julio whispered.

"We just found them lying there," Roberto added.

Inspector Jose Bittencourt stood up and came from behind his official desk. He thought the boys would talk more freely if he was more relaxed with them. The policeman loosened the top button on his shirt, slackened his tie and sat on a low chair next to them.

"It must have been a terrible shock," he said.

Julio leaned forward. "It wasn't. We thought they were sunbathing on the top of the hill."

"Hah!" Roberto argued. "In their raincoats!"

"They might have been sunbathing just their *faces*," Julio pouted.

Roberto was about to make another bitter remark when Inspector Bittencourt cut in. "It's strange, that. They were lying there in their raincoats ... yet it hasn't rained for over a week!"

The boys nodded but didn't have an answer.

"So, let's just go over it once more. You live across the bay in Niteroi town?"

"Yes."

"And you set off this morning to climb Vintem Hill. Why was that?"

"To watch the planes," Julio said. "Vintem Hill's really high and the planes fly just over your head. You can even see the pilots' faces. Sometimes passengers wave to us!"

Inspector Bittencourt knew the planes were flying to and from Santo Dumont Airport in Rio de Janeiro. He also knew that Vintem Hill was over 350 metres above sea level and made a good place to see the whole of Rio across the bay as well as the aircraft landing.

"You saw the planes ..."

"No. We got to the top and saw the dead men," Roberto cut in. "We ran all the way back down. I fell and scraped my knee!" he said, pointing to a large white bandage on his brown skin.

"I see," the policeman nodded. "But did you see anyone else on the hill? When you were on your way to the top did you meet anyone coming down?"

The boys looked at one another. They shook their heads.

"You live at the foot of the hill? Did you know the men?"

Again they shook their heads.

"And you saw nothing unusual?"

Roberto shook his head but Julio opened his mouth then shut it quickly. Jose Bittencourt was a good policeman and he was patient with children. He had four of his own. "No one on the hill the night before? No lights? No signs of someone moving around?"

When he said the word "lights" Julio gave a small jump. Roberto looked at his friend. Julio's head moved slowly up and down. "Yes . . . lights."

"No, Julio!" Roberto squeaked. "He won't believe you!"

The Inspector leaned back. "I like stories. Tell me about the lights. Lights on the hill? Last night?"

Julio bunched his small, grubby hands into fists and began

to talk quickly. "Sometimes there are lights on the hill at night – people go up there to watch for the flying saucers. But there weren't any lights on the hill last night. The only lights we saw last night were the flying saucers up in the sky."

The Inspector folded his hands calmly and said, "Tell me about the flying saucers."

Julio shrugged. "They're like saucers. And they fly."

"He knows that, stupid," Roberto sighed. "Listen, mister, I'll tell you about them. They're green."

"Yellow," his friend cut in.

"Yes . . . greenish–yellow," Roberto admitted. "And . . ."

"Hold on," Inspector Bittencourt said. "If it's dark then how can you see what colour they are?"

"Because they glow," Julio said.

"So, you really see a greenish light in the sky, yes?"

"I suppose so," Julio agreed, though he couldn't see what difference it made.

"And it's red round the outside," Roberto said.

"Orange," Julio corrected.

"Reddish–orange," Roberto said fiercely.

"And how big is it?" the policeman went on.

"As big as one of the aeroplanes that fly into Santo Dumont," Julio said.

"As big as the Maracana Stadium!" Roberto said. That made Julio blink a little then frown doubtfully but he kept quiet.

"And what did this greenish–yellow disc do when you saw it last night?" Inspector Bittencourt went on.

"It sort of drifted to the top of Vintem Hill," Julio said.

"Did it stop there?"

Julio's face creased in a frown. "It must have done. That's how it dropped the two dead bodies off!"

It was the Inspector's turn to blink and frown. "You saw this?"

"No, but that's what Mrs Souza was saying this morning."

Inspector Bittencourt made a note of her name then sucked at the end of the pencil. "Look, boys, you have been wonderful witnesses. I have to get you back to Niteroi soon. I need to talk to some of the detectives who've been working on the case then I'll take you back myself."

"In a police car?" Julio gaped.

"In a police car. Anything you want to see while you're waiting for me?" the policeman smiled.

"The motor-cycles," Roberto breathed and his friend nodded.

When the Inspector had arranged for the two to be entertained for half an hour he walked to the office of the medical examiner on the third floor of the concrete and glass police headquarters. "So how did they die, doctor?"

Doctor Alvarez was sitting behind her desk, leafing through thick medical books. She pushed her dark, heavy hair away from her forehead and then rubbed her tired eyes. "For the first time in my life I have to admit that I don't know. There are no marks of violence on the bodies – they weren't stabbed or beaten or shot – and the stomachs show no sign of the usual poisons. Their hearts were in perfect working order and they weren't drowned, suffocated or strangled."

Inspector Bittencourt sat down heavily. "That's not a lot of help. I don't know if we're looking at suicide, murder or accident."

"Or natural causes," the doctor put in.

"Hardly likely that they'd die at the same time of natural causes."

Doctor Alvarez nodded. "At least I can say they died within

minutes of each other. Sorry I can't be of more help. Two young, healthy men. It's a mystery."

Jose Bittencourt pushed himself wearily to his feet, nodded a brisk goodbye and walked back to his office. Within minutes he'd called the scene-of-crime officers and his detection team into the office. He turned to the scene-of-crime sergeant first – a thin-faced man with a worried expression. "Sorry, sir. Nothing there to help us. I can't see any footprints other than the two boys'. I can't really say if the dead men walked to the top of the hill or if they were dropped there."

The Inspector rolled a pencil between his fingers in irritation. "Alvarez can't tell me how they died, now you're saying you can't tell me *where* they died. Come along, man, give me some help."

The sergeant leaned forward and said, "Officially I cannot commit myself. But, off the record, I have a feeling that they died somewhere else."

"Thank you," Bittencourt said. He looked at the row of officers. "What do we know about the dead men?"

Detective Sergeant Ramon flipped open a notebook and smiled brightly. Ramon was always eager to impress the Inspector. "Their names are Manuel Cruz and Miguel Viana. They live in Campos and they are both television engineers and they were last seen at home going to Rio to buy a car."

Bittencourt thought about the information for a moment. "If they were going to buy a car they'd have needed money. There were only a few cruzeiros in their pockets when they were found. Perhaps they were robbed."

Detective Sergeant Ramon's grin widened and his chest expanded with pride. "I thought of that, sir. I checked at their bank. They took out several thousand cruzeiros when they left Campos but they never reached Rio."

"They were robbed on the way?"

"No, sir. They took a bus and they got off at Niteroi. I asked the Niteroi police to run a check on the raincoats. The men got off the bus and bought the raincoats then set off to climb Vintem Hill."

Inspector Bittencourt was becoming more irritated by the young officer who seemed to know everything. "So, Sergeant Ramon, why did they need raincoats on a scorching hot day?"

Ramon's face fell. "I – I don't know, sir."

"And why were they climbing Vintem Hill?"

"I don't know, sir."

The Inspector took a deep breath. "Detective work is about *motive*, Ramon. Find out about the victim and you find out about the crime. It is *not* about simple facts."

"No, sir."

"But there were other clues, sir," the scene-of-crime officer said.

"What?"

"There were two very rough masks made out of lead. They were very close to the faces of the bodies." He held up two dull grey metal masks moulded into distorted human faces.

"Anything else?"

"Three sheets of paper, Inspector." He showed the senior policeman three clear plastic bags. Each contained a piece of paper – one green and two blue. The first had a complicated formula written on it. It looked like something from a science book. The second was a message. The writing was clear but the message was baffling.

Inspector Bittencourt read it aloud. "Sunday, one pill after meal. Monday, one pill after meal. Tuesday, one pill after meal. Wednesday, one pill lying down." The third sheet said, "4.30 p.m. be at the appointed place. 6.30, swallow pill. Then protect face with metal and wait for signal to show itself."

"There were reports of unidentified flying objects in the area," Ramon said.

"I know about the UFOs, thank you, Ramon," the Inspector snapped. "If you see any little green men then arrest them on suspicion of murder, will you?"

"Yes, sir," the sergeant said brightly.

"That was a joke, Ramon."

"Sorry, sir."

"I want to talk to someone who knew the men. When I find out who they were – what sort of people they were – I'll understand the case."

He rose and walked to the door, snapping orders for his driver to bring a car – and the two boys, Julio and Roberto – round to the main entrance. "Lock the papers in the safe, Ramon," was his final order.

To entertain the boys the Inspector asked the driver to switch on the siren and within minutes they were clear of the city and on to the bridge across the bay to Niteroi. He waved goodbye to the boys and thanked them for their help. Then he headed for Campos and the quiet bungalow where Miguel Viana's father lived.

The man was grey-haired and round-shouldered. He was wearing a grey sweater over a grubby white shirt. "I'm sorry about your son, Mr Viana," the Inspector said as he was shown into the darkened living room and sat on a battered couch.

The old man's watery eyes looked mournfully up at the policeman. "I knew it would end this way. Miguel and Manuel were always interested in aliens ever since they were children. They became television engineers but they were really interested in making transmitters that would send signals to space craft."

"You think they succeeded?" the Inspector asked.

"Of course. They did their experiments in the garage. There were explosions and there were lights but I knew they had succeeded."

"In talking to the aliens?"

"In talking to the aliens. Of course the aliens couldn't let them live. They lured my Miguel to the top of Vintem Hill and killed them."

"Why would they do that, Mr Viana?"

The old man looked at the policeman in wonder. "To silence my son. They killed him because he knew too much!"

"He knew the radio waves to contact them on?"

"Oh, yes. He must have done."

Suddenly Inspector Bittencourt understood the importance of the scrap of paper. It wasn't a formula – it was a calculation of radio wavebands. With that piece of paper a human could talk to a being from another planet. The policeman made a quick apology and excuse to leave. This time the flashing lights and siren were for real, not to entertain two children.

The police car sped back across the bridge and through the Rio streets to Police Headquarters. Detective Sergeant Ramon was leaving as the Inspector rushed in.

"The formula, Ramon! Where is it?"

"You instructed me to place it in the safe, sir, so naturally I placed it ..."

"Let's get it!" Bittencourt cried.

A puzzled Ramon followed the Inspector to the secure room and the duty officer opened the safe. "I just put them in here sir," he said. He reached into the safe and pulled out two plastic envelopes. The papers inside were blue.

"The green one, man. The green one. The one with the formula on it."

The desk officer blushed a little and groped around the steel safe with a shaking hand. "It was there, sir. Sergeant Ramon saw me put it in."

"I did, sir," Ramon agreed.

"So where is it now?"

The officer looked at the Inspector with a mixture of embarrassment and fear. "It can't have gone anywhere, sir ... but it has!"

"There's no power on Earth could have got into that safe and taken that paper," Bittencourt whispered. "No power ... on *Earth*."

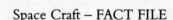

## Space Craft – FACT FILE

In Washington State on 24 June 1947, pilot Kenneth Arnold set out to search for an aircraft that had crashed into the Cascade Mountains. As he looked for wreckage he saw a flash of light and reported later, "I observed, far to my left and to the north, a formation of nine very bright objects coming from the vicinity of Mount Baker, flying very close to the mountain tops and travelling with tremendous speed. I could see no tails on them, and they flew like no aircraft I had seen before ... like a saucer would if you skipped it across the water." When a newspaper reported the story the next day it came up with the phrase "flying saucer" and the name stuck.

Brazil has been called Flying Saucer Alley, there have been so many sightings there. Not all are as deadly as the one in the story. Sightings began soon after the first US reports in 1947. In July of that year, Jose Higgins saw a large metal disc land on curved legs at Sao Paulo. Giant aliens pointed a tube at him and he fled. He turned to look and saw them throwing huge boulders around like tennis balls.

Two weeks later Professor Johannis in Italy

saw a red disc land and two dwarf aliens came out.

The boys in Rio described a yellow-green disc with an orange-red rim. This gives an idea of the problem in believing UFO reports. The machines are all so different.

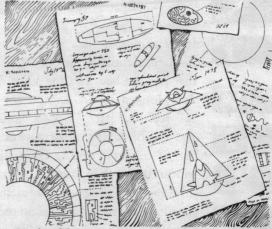

In the fifty years since there have been many reports of UFOs and many describe a circular object. But not all are the same shape, size or colour and not all move in the same way. The alien fliers seem to have more types of space craft than we earthlings have types of motor car. Here are a few . . .

### Shape and size

A 4-metre football (American football or rugby ball – Massachusetts, USA, 1966)
A cone (Indiana, USA, 1973)
A 100-metre-long cigar, 20 metres high (Wyoming, USA, 1976)
A dome about 15 metres across with portholes

(Yorkshire, England, 1978)
A 400-metre boomerang (Arizona, USA, 1981)
A solid black triangle, 70 metres wide, with
blinking lights at each corner (Belgium, 1990)

## Colour

Black bubbles with silver tails (Massachusetts,
USA, 1965)
Glowed with a red light (Scotland, 1971)
A yellowish-whitish ball (Bermuda, 1979)
Glowing orange with a green light at the back,
red lights at the top and bottom and white
headlights (Tennessee, USA, 1980)

## Features

Twelve red lights on surface and searchlight
underneath (Arizona, USA, 1981 )
A flying disc that can shrink to just 50cm, enter
a house and unload a dozen crew members who
are 75 cm tall! (north-east England, 1979)
A beam that can knock humans unconscious
and make them forget the sighting (Maine,
USA, 1975)
A blue beam that can shine on to water and suck
up a supply into the space craft (Hokkaido,
Japan, 1973)
Flashing lights of many colours, like a Christmas
tree (northern Spain, 1974)
A beam can turn a car steering wheel too hot to
touch (Brazil, 1995)

Not only are the space craft varied. So are their pilots. Many witnesses agree that they look generally like humans but some of the differences are great. If these reports are true then there is not another form of intelligent life in the universe ... there are hundreds of forms of intelligent life, and many of them have found our little planet.

The most common alien is the "Grey" but there are many others . . .

## Height
1 metre tall (Augusta, USA, 1973)
"The size of large dolls" with white hair (northern England, 1978)
1 metre 30 cm with green skin (Argentina, 1974)
2 metres 30 cm tall with antennae on the head (Wales, 1981)
2 metres 40 cm tall with a furry body and webbed duck feet (Brazil, 1975)

## Dress
Pointed hoods or breathing masks (Indiana, USA, 1973)

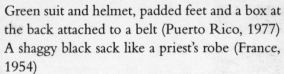      

Green suit and helmet, padded feet and a box at the back attached to a belt (Puerto Rico, 1977)

A shaggy black sack like a priest's robe (France, 1954)

Transparent plastic suits (France, 1954)

Green metal suit (Brazil, 1995)

## Appearance

Round face, large pointed ears, big round blue eyes and no neck (Japan, 1975)

Large head, long slanting eyes, a slit mouth and long chin (France, 1965)

Grey wrinkled skin and a single slit for an eye, crab-claw hands (Mississippi, USA, 1973)

Like rats, with rat ears and mouths like slits (Brazil, 1980)

Like a landmine or a ball with arms (Scotland, 1979)

They look so human they can be mistaken for us; blue-eyed and blond-haired (Florida, USA, 1996)

**Powers**

Flying like Superman (Puerto Rico, 1979)

Hypnotizing humans by pointing a finger at them (Virginia, USA, 1973)

Knock humans over with an invisible force (Russia, 1978)

Speak without "talking" – the voices just happen inside the human's mind (Brazil, 1980)

Bullets bounce off the goblin-like creatures (Kentucky, USA, 1965)

Looks like a little boy but changes to an alien when it steps inside space craft (Britain, 1996)

*Not all aliens are threatening and destructive. It seems that some have nothing but goodwill towards humans. A father and daughter discovered their own Christmas angels in 1979 in Scotland …*

"While shepherds washed their socks by night all seated round a tub, an angel of the Lord came down and gave them all a scrub!" the girl bawled then giggled.

Her father changed gear and the car crawled up the steep hill towards a moonwashed sky. "Katie, you have a voice like a foghorn."

"Foghorns can't sing," she sniffed.

"Neither can you," the man muttered.

The headlights of the car were dim and yellow but the moon was bright enough to show the twisting road and the steep drop to the left.

The roads had been crowded with Christmas shoppers in Edinburgh. Jim Hanson had hoped to make the trip into the highlands in daylight but had been delayed. Now the traffic had vanished – he and his daughter hadn't seen another car for the past twenty minutes – but his tired Mini was struggling to make up for the lost time.

The radio had faded to a stream of crackles and Katie had started to sing to cheer them up. Even the feeble heater didn't want to warm the frosty air and the singing took the girl's mind off her frozen feet.

Jim seemed to read his daughter's mind. "Your mother will have a good fire going in the cottage when we get there."

"Ha! You mean *if* we get there." Katie groaned.

"Don't say that," Jim said sharply. "Once we're at the top of this pass it's downhill most of the way to Fort William."

"Can we stop at the next town?" Katie asked. "Just for some chocolate?"

"Sorry, there's nowhere to stop till we get to Glencoe."

"Is that where we are?" the girl asked. "That's where all those people were massacred, isn't it? We learned about it in history. It was horrible."

Jim laughed. "You've seen Glencoe in the daylight. It's a bleak place even in the summer. In winter snows it must have been miserable. I think I'd rather have been massacred than live there."

The car spluttered, lurched then rumbled on. Jim changed gear again. The lights dimmed just a little more. "Nearly there," he said. He was really trying to convince himself. "There'll be a great view from the top. You'll be able to see the lights of all the villages in the valley below. In fact we can switch the engine off and free-wheel down into Glencoe Village."

The engine picked up and the car speed began to increase. "We're at the top now," the man said and blew his cheeks out in relief.

Katie leaned forward and peered through the screen. "So where are the lights?" she asked. Ahead was a darkness as black as the inside of a mountain.

"Must be the bad weather they forecast for the West of Scotland," Jim muttered and hunched forward over the wheel. Within half a mile they were swallowed by a mist. The road disappeared in front of the weak headlights as it swung right and left. Occasionally the front wheels of the tiny car skidded on the gravel at the edge of the road. Clammy tentacles of mist crept into the front of the car and made the engine cough. Their speed was down to walking pace though they knew they were running downhill. Cold slid through the badly-fitting doors and Katie shivered.

"I wish we'd brought some warm clothes," she said.

"We didn't know we were going to need them," her father groaned. "I thought we'd save the space and pack in the presents."

They went silent for ten minutes as the car groped its way down the pass. "Mum will be worried," the girl said.

"We'll phone when we get to Glencoe," Jim said.

This time Katie didn't say if – it wasn't a joke any longer. Suddenly the road swung to the right, Jim stamped on the brakes and the car skidded. As it slewed around Katie gasped and waited for them to tip over the edge of some steep drop. But Jim had been deceived by a fork in the road. The main road had gone to the right but the minor road had been slightly to the left and he had simply slid on to it. As he knocked the car into reverse there was a wailing from the gearbox and the scream of complaining gears.

The man swore and said, "That remote rod has finally gone."

"We're stuck here?"

"Not exactly. It just means I can't reverse. I can only go forward. Where does this road take us to?"

Katie opened the door and peered at a signpost. "Put the main beam on, Dad," she said. She read the sign and jumped back into the car as the icy wind cut through her thin sweatshirt and school blazer. "The Glencoe Visitors' Centre."

Jim nodded. "I know it. It's a climb of a couple of miles into the hills but we can phone from there. Maybe stay the night and head for the cottage tomorrow."

"Nice way to spend Christmas," Katie sighed.

The road seemed endless. The windscreen wipers moaned as they swept the thin mist off the screen. Then a white ridge grew at the bottom of each sweep. "It's snowing."

"I'm dreaming of a white Christmas," Katie sang softly and

her father laughed.

"Keep your eyes peeled for the entrance to the centre," he said.

Katie stared at the swirling patterns in front of the car and cried, "There's a light!"

Jim dabbed at the brakes but the wheels seemed to lock and the car shot over the slippery surface. It hit a large stone at the edge of the road and tipped into a shallow ditch. Jim tore his door open to see the damage, he stepped out and gave a cry as he disappeared from Katie's sight.

She jumped out on to the road and cried, "Dad!"

There was a groaning from his side of the car. She hurried round in front of the fading headlights and found him. He'd stepped on to the crumbling edge of the road and tumbled into the ditch. "Can you get up, Dad?"

"No . . . my ankle . . . turned on it . . . think it's broken."

She slid down the small embankment till she stood over him. She tugged frantically at his elbow, sweating in spite of the bitter cold. "Come on, Dad. You'll freeze out here!"

"Go to the visitors' centre," he groaned. "It can't be far."

She looked into the darkness. The mist was thinner but the dark was as thick as smoke. In the shadow of the steep valley sides even the moon was blotted out, "I won't even be able to see the road under my feet."

She took her father's hand and tugged. The shock seemed to be making him faint and he was a dead weight. After a minute of tugging she gave up the struggle, threw herself on top of him and clutched him tightly, trying to share the little warmth they had. "Someone will come along soon," she whispered. Then as her arms began to turn numb she started to sing a carol which was the nearest thing to a prayer she could think of. "While shepherds watched their flocks by night, all seated on the ground, an angel of the Lord came down and glory shone around."

As she slipped into sleep she could feel a trembling at first. Maybe a vehicle on the road. She raised her head stiffly. There was the light again. The one she'd seen from the car. But it wasn't at the side of the road, it was above the road. And it was moving. Like some brilliant Christmas star in the darkness it swept slowly and smoothly along the road. Then the beam of light from the star struck Katie's blue-white face and stopped.

"Help!" she tried to cry but nothing came from her trembling lips. It wasn't a helicopter, because it was too quiet. There was only a deep humming and it was that noise that was making the ground tremble slightly. Behind the glare of the light she could make out the shape of some disc with a dome on top. It was as large as a house.

Then a square of pale green light opened in the side of the disc as if someone had opened a door. Dark silhouettes appeared in the doorway and walked down a ramp towards her.

Katie was dazzled by the light but she could see they were

human in shape but incredibly thin with stick-insect limbs. On their heads they wore some kind of helmet. They didn't seem to feel the cold though they wore just thin, black uniforms.

There were three of them. One stretched a twig-hand towards her and touched her forehead. The voice seemed to be there inside her head saying, "You are safe."

Another creature ran a hand down her father's leg and she sensed a message saying, "Ligament damage. No break."

The thin-limbed creature slid its arms under Katie and picked her up as if she were weightless. Its companion did the same to her father while the third one opened the car door and let her sit on the seat. Jim Hanson sat with his legs out of the open door and the creature was passing a bottle to him. Jim nodded.

"Dad?" Katie whispered.

"It wants me to drink this," he said hoarsely.

"I think they want to help," was all she could say.

He drank it then passed the bottle to Katie. She didn't hesitate but drank the sweet, warming liquid. Her body seemed to melt like a snowman in July as warmth flooded through her.

"It's killed the pain in my leg too," her father smiled.

"But we're still in trouble," she groaned.

There was a soft tap on her window and a twig-finger scraped at it. Katie unfastened the catch and slid the window open. The finger rested on her forehead and she closed her eyes to concentrate. "It says we have to sit still, not move and not be afraid."

Jim Hanson gave a short laugh. "We haven't any choice."

"It wants to know where we're going," she went on. "Shall I tell it the visitors' centre?"

The man shrugged. "Why don't they just give us a lift all the way to Arisaig?"

Why not? she thought. She closed her eyes and pictured the village on the map. Moments later the creature broke contact and walked away from the car. It disappeared towards the glowing green doorway in a curious, clumsy stride.

"They're leaving us," she cried.

The searchlight flickered off and the disc began to move towards the car. When it was directly over the roof thin beams of light spread from under the craft and wrapped themselves around the car. There was a small jolt as the craft lifted up and took the car with it. The next five minutes were the most magical Katie had ever known. They rose high above the valley and its mist so the country lay beneath them like a moonlit map. To the west the sea glinted silver and towns and villages sparkled with street lights and Christmas illuminations. Here on the coast the sea breeze had cleared the mist away.

They had no feeling of movement yet the ground flew beneath them as if they were riding on some magic carpet. The brilliant streamers of light that were Fort William slipped by and then tiny ribbons of village lights came up to them.

They touched the road again as softly as a falling snowflake. The beams of power that held them snapped off. Katie squinted through the window and watched the disc climb with incredible speed then stop. A pinprick of light among the stars. It hovered there, watching.

The car was facing downhill. Katie recognized the school to the right. She pointed it out to her father. He nodded and allowed the car to roll down the hill into Arisaig village and the cottage.

Katie stepped out of the car and the cottage door swung

open. "You're a little late, what kept you?" her mother grinned.

Jim hobbled from the car towards the warm light from the windows.

The girl looked up at the stars. One glowed a little brighter and a little more green. "Happy Christmas!" she called.

"Happy Christmas?" her mother said, puzzled. "Who are you talking to?"

"I didn't used to believe in angels," Katie said as she helped her father into the house.

The man turned and looked at the steady green light. "No," he said. "Not angels."

Creatures from Heaven and Hell –
FACT FILE

Some ufologists believe that aliens did not just appear in 1947 with the Kenneth Arnold "flying saucer" sighting. They believe aliens have been with us for thousands or even tens of thousands of years. A Native American Indian tribe, the Oglala Sioux, believed they could travel to other worlds where they would be taken apart and put back together . . . very similar to experiences of modern people who say they've been abducted.

Perhaps other ancient people saw aliens but did not believe they were creatures from another planet. Perhaps they saw them as gods . . . or angels or devils. After all, just like a god they could have appeared from the sky, had incredible powers and they could kill or cure any human they came into contact with.

Did aliens appear on Earth thousands of years ago and were they mistaken for supernatural beings? Were the Greys our heroes and the cruel "Reptile" people the dragons of the old story? Here are some ideas that support the idea . . .

**1.** Where did ancient people get the idea of

devils and hell? Some ufologists have said that the Earth is hollow and aliens live beneath the earth – hell. There is a hole at the North Pole. Flying saucers come and go through this hole. Maybe they took some humans there once and the humans returned with stories of the "underworld".

**2.** One type of reported alien is more like a ghost than a solid being. They appear and disappear wherever they want, change shape to anything they like and drift above the ground rather than walk. If an ancient person saw one of those you can understand how they saw it as a god. The chief Greek god was Zeus – he could appear as a bird or an animal and blast people with a thunderbolt ... or was he a shape-changing alien with a laser cannon?

**3.** Old spirits of the woods were known as elves or brownies. These are the size of children and

wear a suit that is made in one piece – just like a Grey, in fact. "Devils" were often small and ugly – look at the stone devils carved along the gutters of old cathedrals. The carvings are known as gargoyles. Were the designers working from sketches of devils – or from sightings of aliens?

**4.** Ancient people believed in giants – did they in fact see some of the huge aliens that have been reported in modern times? In the 1950s an archaeologist visited the Mayan pyramids in Mexico and said the stones were too huge to have been moved by humans. He became a leading writer on aliens. He believed that the Mexican Indians had the help of alien giants – probably helped by the powerful lifting forces of something like a flying saucer.

**5.** People of earlier times were afraid of babies being kidnapped by wicked "fairies". They often left a wooden doll or an ugly little creature in its place. Were these little kidnappers in fact aliens who were abducting the children just as modern aliens are said to abduct adults? And were the doll-creatures in fact robot replacements or young aliens?

**6.** The Egyptians were a simple farming people until they were organized by a powerful group of leaders known as pharaohs. But archaeologists have discovered that the pharaohs

were not just peasants with power – they were different. They had larger skulls ... like the Greys. And they had the idea for huge constructions, the Pyramids. Were they invading humans who took control of the peasants ... or were they from another planet altogether?

**7.** In the story of the Christian Nativity the Three Wise Men follow a bright star in the sky to find the infant Jesus. Were they in fact seeing a UFO hovering in the sky? And was the super-human Jesus in fact an alien? Some people have said that's what they believe. The Old Testament of the bible describes a vision of the prophet Ezekiel which sounds familiar to ufologists: *As I looked a stormy wind came out of the North and a great cloud with brightness round about it and fire flashing continually. And from the midst of it came the likeness of four living creatures. They had the form of men but each had four faces and four wings. As I looked at them I saw a wheel upon the earth beside the creatures, one each, and when the creatures went the wheels went beside them and when the creatures rose from the earth the wheels rose.*

**8.** Aliens have been accused of killing cattle and other farm animals. So were witches in historical times. But were they all human witches? Or were some of them aliens disguised as humans? And did they go out destroying cattle just as today's aliens are said to? And did

they have small jet-packs for moving around the countryside? And, in the darkness, did the simple country folk mistake the jet-pack for something familiar ... a broomstick, perhaps?

**9.** There have always been stories of mysterious animals that appear and terrify humans but disappear when they are hunted. Are these sea monsters, abominable snowmen and big-foot creatures in fact aliens? Is the Loch Ness Monster a visitor from another planet that lives in the loch on its regular trips to Earth?

**10.** Shape-changing creatures are said to live among humans but then change back to their horrifying selves at certain times. These creatures have become known as vampires and werewolves. Are they in fact aliens? It's strange that vampires – like the Greys who kidnap – take blood. And isn't it curious that so-called werewolves are affected by a body in space ... a full moon?

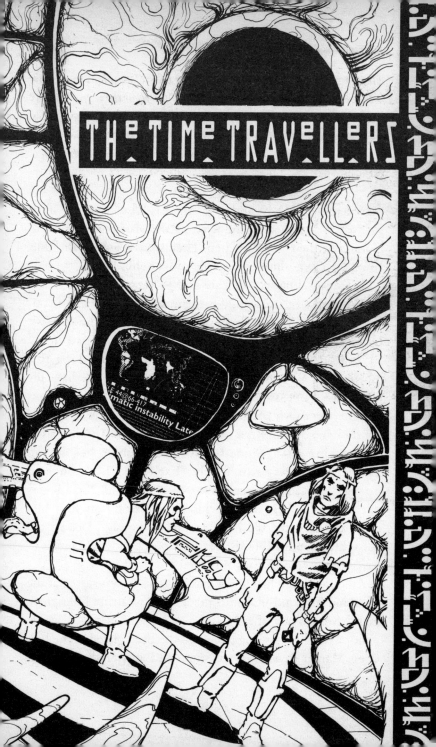

*There are two problems with UFOs and their alien pilots. If they are from a distant planet then how could they travel all the way to Earth? And, if they are from a totally different world to ours, how come they look so much like human beings? This story, from Somerset, England, in 1995, gives one explanation which answers both of these problems …*

"Good morning, boys and girls," the head teacher said. Thirty pairs of eyes turned to the front of the class but none were looking at their head teacher. They were fixed on the thin young man who limped into the room behind her.

The head went on, "You are doing a class project on UFOs and I promised that I would bring in someone to talk to you. Mr Gregory Martin here is a member of the British Unidentified Flying Object Research Association … BUFORA … and he's kindly agreed to come along this morning to talk to you. I know you have many questions for him and I'll not waste any more of your time. I'll hand you straight over to Mr Martin." The head teacher took her seat at the desk next to the class teacher and watched with interest.

The thin man limped across to a chair beside the blackboard and sat down heavily. "Excuse me. I have suffered from a paralysed leg since I was a child," he said. "Standing is uncomfortable." He wiped a thin film of sweat from his white brow and clutched the handkerchief nervously. "I could tell you a little about BUFORA but I expect you would prefer to have your own questions answered."

A boy with red hair and a mass of freckles was sitting at the back and his hand shot into the air. "How many little green men have you seen then?"

Some of the class sniggered and the head glared at the boy. Greg Martin gave a pained smile and answered, "I expect there are many like you who don't believe in alien beings. Why is that?"

"Cos I've never seen one," the red-haired boy answered.

"Have you ever seen Charles Dickens?"

"He's dead!"

"Has anyone here seen him?"

"Why ... no!"

"But you believe he exists?"

"Course."

The ufologist raised a weary shoulder. "Believing is not always seeing. And seeing is not always believing. What is your name?"

"Jason Capstick," the boy said.

"Then let's have a deal, Jason. I'll tell you what *I* believe and *you* will listen. When I've finished you can make up your own mind. OK?"

Jason nodded. "OK."

"As you can see, my leg is weak. I have never had a strong body. But nature is strange. Instead nature gave me a strong *mind*. When I was your age strange things began to happen ... radios switched on by themselves, television sets changed channels when I walked into a room and one day a baby's pram spun round as I walked past it."

"What's that got to do with little green men?" Jason asked.

Greg Martin took a deep breath. "If your head teacher here, Miss Grayson, said the school was on fire you would believe her and get out as quickly as possible – if this girl in the front row told you three times in one day that the school was on fire, and lied every time, then you may not believe her. You need to understand the person telling the story as well as the story."

Jason folded his arms. "Fair enough," he said.

"I became interested in UFOs when I started seeing them back in 1993."

A girl in the front row raised a hand. "What did it look like?"

"It was the shape of a ball – not the sort of flying 'saucer' you'd expect. I'd got out of bed to use the bathroom about two in the morning. Suddenly the room was lit by a brilliant light. I looked out of the window and saw it hovering there for maybe four seconds. Then it began to move. It didn't make a sound. It just vanished over the roof tops."

"How big was it?" a long-haired girl on his left asked.

Greg Martin winced. "That's the hard part to believe ... you see, it was the size of a football!"

The statement caused a sensation in the class. From gasps of disbelief to laughter and cries of, "Aliens couldn't be that small," and "I never knew aliens played football!"

The head teacher stood up and glared at the class. The noise subsided. Greg Martin went on, "I know it's hard to believe, but think about it. The creatures we call aliens must be enormously advanced beings to travel the way they do. They could well have the technology to shrink everything – imagine the power they'd save."

Some of the brighter ones in the class understood this and nodded. "The sighting seemed to be imprinted on my brain. Even when I went back to bed and closed my eyes I could still see it. My head was throbbing and my eyes were burning."

"My dad gets like that when he's been drinking," a boy said in a loud whisper. The ufologist heard him.

"That's a fair point. But sorry, I don't drink."

The class smiled and leaned forward a little to hear his story. "It wasn't till the next night that I had my vision. Again, this is not easy to believe, but I can only tell you what I experienced. I can't explain it all. I went to bed and closed my eyes. When I opened them I found I was no longer in my bed."

"Sleep-walking," a girl muttered to her friend.

"You were dreaming," Jason put in.

"Do you dream, Jason?" the man asked.

"Course."

"What did you dream last night?"

"Can't remember."

"Exactly! Dreams slip away and fade. But real experiences stay with you forever. You can believe that what happened was a dream. I am sure it was not."

"So what *did* happen?" the red-haired boy asked.

"I found myself in the control room of some sort of enormous flying machine. I could feel it moving and trembling with the force of its motors. The room was flooded in blue light. There was a desk in the centre with hundreds of control switches and lights ..."

"Sounds like something from Star Trek," a boy with glasses giggled, but the rest of the class ignored him. They were becoming hooked on the man's story.

"There were three humans at the control desk watching a large screen in front of them. At first they didn't seem to notice I was there. I walked towards them and heard them talking about the pictures they'd been watching."

"Hang on!" Jason cried. "How did you know what they were talking about? Little green Martians don't speak English!"

"Good question. But I have to tell you they were neither Martian nor little and green. They were as human as you are!"

"Jason's not human!" somebody chuckled.

Greg Martin smiled and went on, "I was a bit disappointed.

They looked so *ordinary*. They had long hair, tanned skin and bright blue eyes but if they walked into the room now you would believe they were human. It would only be if you looked at their hands you'd notice they had no fingernails."

"What were they wearing?" a girl with a pony-tail asked.

"Grey uniforms with a badge on the front pocket. The captain – the tallest one in the middle – had a silver band round his head. They all had dark grey boots with a blue stripe across the front."

"Why didn't they see you?" Miss Grayson asked suddenly.

"But they did once the screen went blank. They turned and looked at me with no surprise as if they knew I'd been there all the time. I reached out to touch one and my hand passed straight through him."

"Aww!" Jason Capstick groaned. "It's a ghost story, not a UFO story."

"I know what you mean, Jason, and in a way it is. I was shocked by my hand passing through the leader and they explained very quickly. They were humans from Earth and very much alive. But all I could see of them were projections."

"Holograms!" someone exclaimed.

"Exactly," Greg agreed. "We could see each other but we weren't actually in the same place at the same time."

Jason Capstick was sitting on the edge of his desk. "But this is silly," he objected. "Even the Americans can't make holograms you can talk to ... not yet, anyway."

Greg relaxed and grinned. "Exactly, Jason! You've solved the mystery!"

"I have?"

"You have!"

"What did I say?"

"You said, 'Not yet'. It's something that is coming. Within

a hundred years people will mix with other people from around the world without leaving their own homes."

"But we aren't living a hundred years from now," the red-haired boy complained.

"We aren't . . . but the people I met are!"

The class went silent for several seconds. Then Jason Capstick clapped his hands once. "Time travellers! That explains everything! You are saying that UFOs don't come from other planets ... they come from this planet a few hundred years in the future!"

"That's what I believe," the ufologist agreed.

"And the aliens people see aren't aliens at all – they're humans from the future?"

"Exactly!"

"And they visit us the way we might go back in a time machine to visit the Battle of Hastings or something?"

"Yes."

Jason Capstick was excited by the idea and his green eyes were glowing. "So why did they come back to visit you?"

Greg rose stiffly and said, "That is the sad part, I'm afraid. They are travelling back to this time because the Earth is still inhabitable. In the future mankind will destroy the planet with pollution. By the year AD 3600 there will be no plant life, no ocean life and no animals. The atmosphere is choked by a black cloud of pollution. The ice caps have melted and flooded most of the great cities. Millions of humans have died. Only the time travellers have survived by coming back to our age and breathing the air before it becomes unbreathable."

The class looked at the man open-mouthed and silent. "It will not happen in your lifetime," he said gently, "but it will begin in your lifetime . . . if you let it. The time travellers tell me that only serious efforts to cut pollution will save the Earth. But you have to start now before it's too late!"

Jason for once raised a hand as he said slowly and thoughtfully, "So we can change the future? This flooded Earth and extinct animals might not happen?"

"That's correct."

"But if these people come from the future then they know it already has happened!" the boy argued.

"It's what's called a paradox," Miss Grayson put in.

Somewhere down the corridor a bell jangled harshly and sounds told of classes moving on to their next lesson. This class didn't move.

The head teacher stood up and spoke quietly. "Mr Martin has given us a lot to think about. Not aliens in flying saucers but humans warning us about our future. Thank you, Mr Martin, for coming in and facing the questions."

"Thanks for giving me the chance," he replied. "I believe that is what the crew of that UFO wanted me to do. The old don't believe me – that doesn't matter – but it would be good to think the young will listen. Thank you all," he finished.

As the class filed out of the room they were subdued and thoughtful. The boy with glasses turned to Jason Capstick. "You believe all that, Jase?"

"It makes you think," he replied carefully. "It makes you think."

## UFO Travel – FACT FILE

A hundred years ago a writer called H G Wells wrote a sensational book called *The Time Machine*. Within thirty years the great mathematician, Albert Einstein, said that time travel was in fact possible.

Modern scientists have said it is *not* possible – then, in 1996, changed their minds and said it *was* possible!

Time and space are linked to each other. Travel through one and you travel through the other.

Walk to school and you arrive at a different time from when you set off.

Stand still for a minute and you have in fact moved a vast distance because the Earth is turning as well as going round the Sun and moving across the galaxy.

If you can solve the problem of controlling time then you can control space. Go to anywhere you want on Earth – or anywhere in the universe.

How can creatures travel through time and space? Have aliens solved this problem? And does that explain how they can come to Earth while we cannot return the visit?

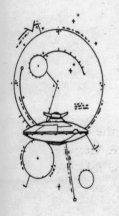

**FACT FILE**

## Wormholes

Imagine space is the shape of an apple. Travel from the stalk of the apple down to the bottom of the apple and you move over the surface. But, if you were a maggot, you could find a quicker way to get from one end to the other. You travel *through* the apple. Much shorter.

There are billions of wormholes in space, scientists say. Some are minute and only open for a tiny fraction of a second. But if we can find these wormholes and create a machine to hold the doorways open then we could travel down them.

## The folded universe

Take a sheet of paper. Mark "A" at the top of the paper and "B" at the bottom edge. Measure the distance from "A" to "B". Now fold the paper so "A" touches "B". The distance

between the two has shrunk so much it has vanished.

If "A" is Earth and "B" is a distant planet then you can travel the length of the paper – hundreds of years even if you travel at the speed of light – or you can "fold" space so "A" is next to "B" and step straight from Earth on to the alien planet.

All you need is a space "folding" machine. No one has invented one yet but many have tried. It works by trying to control gravity – the force that keeps your feet on the ground.

*Many ufologists believe that UFOs are alien space craft flown by extra-terrestrial beings (ETs). When people argue that flying saucers would be recorded by government and military tracking systems, the ufologists say they are. They say the governments of the world know all about UFOs . . .*

I'm tired of it all now. I've talked to the newspapers, the UFO specialists, writers, scientists and complete strangers who track me down and ask me questions.

I've had enough. I will tell my story to you one last time. I will give you every fact I remember, you can print it ... then go away. I never want to hear from UFO watchers again. Is that a deal? In that case I'll tell my story just once more.

If I was in court I guess I'd say, "I swear that the evidence I shall give shall be the truth, the whole truth and nothing but the truth, so help me God." I've got a bible here and I'm resting my right hand on it as I speak. You see it? I'll even swear on my mother's grave that what I saw and heard is true. Why would I lie?

OK, here goes. My name is Robert Charles Savage – though I've always been known as Rob. Back in October 1975, when this UFO thing happened, I was 27 years old. I was living here in Bracebridge, Ontario, Canada and I was a carpenter.

On 7 October 1975, I was away working on a new office block when I got a call from my sister, Mary. Now, let me get this right. She called me some time in the afternoon. The site foreman said there was a call for me and I went down to the site office to take it. It was Mary. Now Mary's a level-headed woman and I knew she wouldn't call me away unless she had a very good reason.

"Rob," she said. "I don't want to worry you but there's an

orange glow coming from over by your barn. I'm worried that there may be a fire."

Now Mary has a small plot of land next to mine – we each have about forty acres – and we keep an eye on one another's property when one of us is away. Why didn't she telephone the fire service? Hell, I don't know. I guess she didn't want to call them out if she was wrong about the fire. Why didn't she go across and take a closer look? Hell, I don't know. You'll have to ask her that. All I can do is tell you my story as I saw it. OK?

OK. I get the call from Mary, ask the site foreman if I can finish early because there may be a problem back home, and I jump into my car for the four-mile journey home. That's right, I owned '69 Buick Riviera and Mary knew I'd be home in five minutes from the town out to our place. It would have taken her longer to walk across to investigate. I guess that's why she called me first.

Now, where was I? Oh, yeah. It's a narrow road, not much better than a dirt track, but I made good time. Nearly took a gatepost off skidding into my front yard and I drove straight across to the barn. I can't tell you how happy I was to see Mary had been wrong. There was no fire. But I was a little worried that the few cows I have had all run as far away to the other side of the field as possible. And the dog didn't bark. I checked inside the house and saw he was hiding under the table.

That's when I decided to go and see Mary. Something had happened to scare the animals but it wasn't a fire. I was hoping she'd be able to help me. Anyway, I climbed back into the car and drove out on to the road again. I wasn't in such a hurry then ... and it's just as well. I should explain, the road twists and turns and there are a few blind corners where a tree or a dip in the road means you can't see what's round the next corner. I guess I was doing about forty miles an hour when I came round the corner and saw the road was totally blocked.

I jammed a foot on the brake and the tail of the car swung round and nearly put me in the ditch.

What was on the road? You might well ask. It was a large disc. Yeah, lots of people have asked me if it was a flying saucer. I guess it must have been. There's no other way to describe it.

Size? Wide enough to block a country road – maybe twice as wide as my car is long. High? Again, about twice as high as a car.

The colour? I guess you'd call it a dull silver – almost the colour of lead. Special features? Well, I don't reckon I can say. The saucer thing must have seen me coming and it was up in the air before I'd really finished skidding to a stop. Now I know the British have those Harrier jump-jets that take off straight up into the air, but I've seen films of them. They don't rise any quicker than a helicopter. This flying saucer thing jumped up like some kind of jack-in-the-box. It was incredible!

It shook me, I can tell you, and I've seen some strange things in my time – served a spell in Vietnam but I never saw a flying ship like that before or since.

I was shaking so much I reached for a pack of cigarettes but my hand was trembling too much to light one. In the end I gave up and started the engine. Why had I switched it off? I hadn't. I guess it stalled when I skidded.

No, no. I didn't keep going to Mary's house. I guess I didn't want her to see me that shaken up. She's always looked up to me as her big brother and I was kind of ashamed that I was just some quivering plate of Jell-O. I decided to head back home, make myself a coffee and call her on the telephone. I turned the car, went back round the bend, accelerating pretty fast, and that's when I had my second shock. There was something standing in the road. A weird little feller, standing there, looking up at the sky so he didn't see me coming.

Looking back I guess the ship had taken off so quickly he'd gotten left behind. But at the time all I thought was I was going to kill some kid in the middle of the road. That's right – he was no bigger than a ten-year-old boy. I hit the brakes and slid straight into him. You ever hit someone in your car? Sickening. I just sat in the driver's seat – something they call shock, isn't it? I couldn't make my legs move to get out and look at the body.

I just stared ahead through the windscreen and then I saw a hand reach up on to the bonnet. I'll swear he only had four fingers. Then a second hand and then a face. He was wearing some kind of helmet like divers do. I could see his face. Big dark eyes and no nose to speak of. He just stared at me for a couple of seconds then turned away and ran to the side of the road. There's a high cattle fence there and I waited for him to climb it. But he didn't. He just placed one hand on a fence post and hopped over like he was weightless. It reminded me of Neil Armstrong walking on the moon. Weird.

Where did he go? He ran off across the field and towards the woods on the hill top. That was the last I saw of him.

Now, as you know, I told my wife the story and the press got a hold of it. Within two days I was doing interviews with press and television and radio and those UFO spotters. It got so I wasn't getting any work done for a week.

But after two weeks things quietened down some and life went back to normal.

Now that's not the weirdest part of the story. It was a year later that one of those UFO watchers came to me and said some Canadian government officials had been in touch with him. They wanted to contact me and talk to me. I thought they may be interested in hearing about this – after all, Canada was as good as being invaded by these little fellers.

But the first thing they did was send me for a full medical examination – and they were quite happy to pay me for the time I lost at work. Then Ontario police arrived with three military officers. The cops said they wanted to talk to me and I said, "Fine". One was in the Canadian forces but the other two were from the USA.

As I say, I thought they'd want to ask questions, but they didn't. They seemed to have read every interview I'd ever given and they knew a hell of a lot about the incident. They didn't come to ask me questions – they came to answer them!

First, they said, they wanted to apologize for the accident. It was caused by a malfunction on an alien space craft. It had landed on our road for repairs and, just as I guessed, the little feller in the diver's helmet got left behind when I appeared and they took off quickly. They asked if I had any questions and I said, "How do you know what happened?" and one of the US officers said, "Because the aliens told us!"

I guess I was dumbstruck by that. "You are in

communication with them!" I cried.

"We are," the Canadian officer said. "The US and Canadian governments have been in touch with aliens since 1943. We have learned a lot from them and I can assure you they are quite friendly."

Now I know there are a hundred questions I should have asked, but I was just too amazed to think straight. They said they kept this information quiet because they didn't want the public to panic and start wild stories about an invasion. They said the governments would release information about the contacts when they were good and ready.

Why did they tell me this? I think it was simply that they wanted to apologize to me for the shock I'd suffered. They wanted me to know that there was nothing to worry about, I wasn't going crazy and I didn't imagine the whole affair.

No, they didn't tell me I had to keep quiet about their visit . . . that's why I'm telling you this.

Yeah, I know the government denies this story . . . the officers said they would . . . but it's true. I'll swear on that same bible that they visited me.

For now I just want to be left alone. I'm happy. I won't go around telling the world that we're being invaded by aliens. I'll just put my trust in God and the government. You'll see . . . one of these days the government will make an announcement. When they're good and ready they'll tell the world that we've been living with aliens for fifty years and they don't mean us any harm.

If you ask me that makes me feel good. It feels good to know that we're not alone in the universe. Good to know that these little grey men are on our side.

Now . . . if you'll excuse me . . . it's supper time and I've told you everything I can remember. You can publish it or you can laugh at it. I don't mind. All I want is for you to tell the world it's the end of the story as far as I'm concerned.

But I'll answer no more questions . . . hell, I won't even answer the door. And, talking about doors, it's over there. If you don't mind you can close it on your way out.

Good night and God bless.

## The Cover-ups – FACT FILE

Many ufologists are convinced, like Robert Charles Savage, that the governments of the world know all about alien landings and alien accidents. They send secret agents round to keep witnesses like Savage quiet.

The Roswell crash is the most famous example of the government plotting to hide the truth from the public. The trouble is there are other explanations for the crash which are just as believable.

If you believe the ufologists then there were *sixteen* UFO crashes in the five years between 1947 and 1952. Sixteen. Don't these aliens ever have to take driving tests? How come they can be so careless? And how come they *all* happened in the USA?

In studying UFOs you always have to look for the most likely explanation of a sighting because that is usually the truth. In the US crashes the following are all possible . . .

**1. A weather balloon.** This is the story that the Air Force broadcast. Many weather balloons, made of a silvery foil, were being sent up from Roswell at that time. It is the most

likely explanation. There was no cover-up. The government told the truth about the wreckage.

**2. Test rocket.** White Sands rocket testing ground is under a hundred miles from Roswell. It was early days and many crashed shortly after take-off. The government arranged to cover up the details of the crash because at that time the rocket tests were top secret. The government invented the weather balloon story.

**3. Space rocket.** The Americans had begun a space exploration programme at White Sands. The rocket scientists used monkeys in thin grey flying suits. The monkey bodies were recovered for examination where mortician Glen Dennis was consulted on their preservation but thrown out of the autopsy building. They were the little Greys seen by witnesses. Again the government covered up the secret testing to keep Soviet spies away.

**4. Japanese bomb balloon.** Towards the end of World War II the Japanese launched over 9000 balloons with high explosive bombs attached. They were released and allowed to drift across the Pacific to land on North America. A few actually got through and started small fires. One could have landed on the ranch and lain there on the remote prairie for two years. The government covered the truth to

stop the public panicking at the thought of these bombs lying all over the USA.

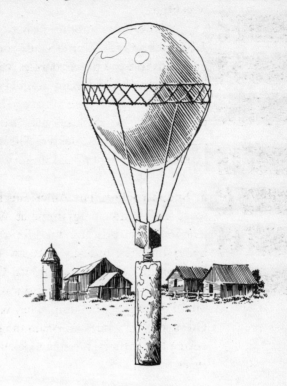

**5. US secret weapon.** Witnesses said they heard a crash during a thunderstorm on 2 July 1947. It is possible that the lightning destroyed not an alien craft but a top secret American war plane. Such a plane would be tested in the emptiest skies the Air Force could find – over the plains of New Mexico. The damaged bodies of the crew may have been found and taken back to Roswell for examination and secret

burial. The government wanted to hide the failure from the public.

Or . . .

A UFO from another planet crash landed at Roswell.

What do you think? Which is the most likely explanation?

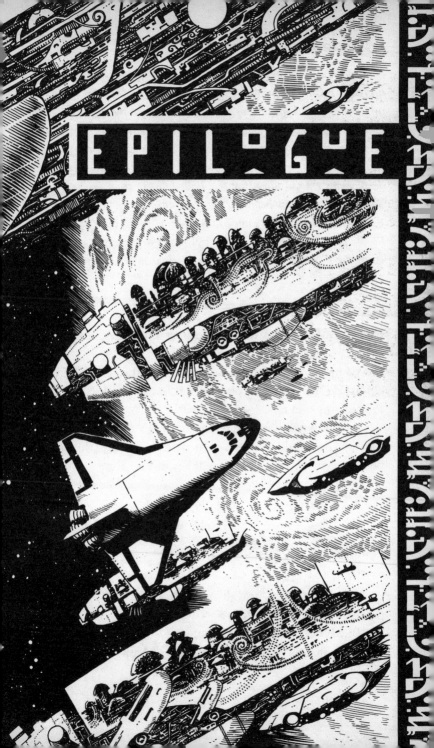

*Is there life on other planets? For years scientists said it was extremely unlikely. But in August 1996 a meteorite from Mars was examined under a powerful microscope and the fossils of tiny organisms were found. Very simple life had existed on Mars billions of years ago! It was called the most important scientific discovery of the century. Then, just a week later, photographs of one of Jupiter's moons showed that deep oceans existed there that could allow life to grow.*

*The disbelievers now believe it — life on other planets is possible.*

*Of course, that's not the same as saying an alien life form has evolved, left its planet and discovered our Earth. To believe that you have to study the stories of UFOs. Here is one final story to help you make up your mind. . .*

## Date: 22 April 1996
## Place: Burnhope Village, County Durham, England

We sit in the cricket pavilion and watch the rain fall from a colourless sky. We can't play until it has stopped so we sit on the balcony and talk.

I've known Brian for ten years. He's the most sensible person you could ever wish to meet. He's not the sort of person to make up stories or tell lies just for fun.

"So what are you writing at the moment?" he asks.

"A book called *True UFO Stories*," I say.

He nods. "Ah, yes. There are plenty of those about," he says.

"Stories or UFOs?" I laugh.

"Both," he says.

"Yes, but they're not all true," I argue. "Some are quite fantastic nonsense and some are plain lies."

"But UFOs exist," he says quietly.

I look at him. "How do you know?" I ask.

He leans forward and looks across the cricket field to the distant woods where I thought I'd seen a UFO as I was starting the book. There is nothing there now. "I was in the RAF in the 1950s," he says. "I did a lot of work on radar. We used to sit and watch the screens for anything unusual entering British air space."

"We were worried about a Russian invasion then." I nod.

"We often used to track things that couldn't be identified," he goes on. "They moved down the country at a tremendous speed – far faster than any aircraft that had ever been invented."

"Your radar machines weren't faulty, were they?"

He shakes his head. "We reported it to the next sector and they tracked it through their air space ... then they passed it on to the next station and so on. The RAF radar crews followed these things all the way down the country. We can't all have had the same fault on the machines."

The rain has stopped and the players are moving back towards the pitch. A hole in the cloud lets a patch of blank sky appear. "Believe what you like," he shrugs. "But I know that there are UFOs out there because I've seen the proof with my own eyes."

The clouds are rolling away quickly now in a fresh breeze. We can look up to a rain-washed blue sky.

An empty sky . . . perhaps.

# TRUE

HORROR
**GHOST**
MONSTER
**SURVIVAL**
SHARK
**CRIME**
DETECTIVE
**SPORT**

# STORIES

# SERIOUSLY

# WEIRD

# TRUE STORIES

Green children, unexplained time slips,
strange stone circles, mysterious beasts
. . . nine incredible tales and over a
hundred weird facts.

**Prepare to be seriously amazed.**